CONTEMPORARY LIVING SPACE

GINGKO PRESS

CONTEMPORARY LIVING SPACE

ISBN 978-1-58423-523-1

First Published in the United States of America by
Gingko Press by arrangement with
Sandu Publishing Co., Ltd.

Text edited by Gingko Press.

Gingko Press, Inc.
1321 Fifth Street
Berkeley, CA 94710 USA
Tel: (510) 898 1195
Fax: (510) 898 1196
Email: books@gingkopress.com
www.gingkopress.com

Copyright © 2013 by Sandu Publishing
First published in 2013 by Sandu Publishing

Sponsored by Design 360°
– Concept and Design Magazine

Edited and produced by
Sandu Publishing Co., Ltd.
Book design, concepts & art direction by
Sandu Publishing Co., Ltd.
sandu.publishing@gmail.com
www.sandupublishing.com

Cover project by Hiroyuki Shinozaki Architects

Printed and bound in China

PREFACE

BY
IÑIGO BEGUIRISTAIN

Contemporary Living Space showcases some of the best residential interiors designed in recent years by renowned professionals worldwide. I must confess that when I was asked to write a forward, my first inclination was to write something generic. I was about to address the task when I was interrupted by a soft melody – the whisper of the works assembled in this particular score. It subtly attracted my attention and prompted a brief walk through the images of the extraordinary projects included in the book, awakening my curiosity. My purpose was suddenly truncated.

I perceived elements of newness and I attempted to overcome gravity and take the necessary distance that any critical analysis requires: exactly the same distance the designer requires with regard to his paper – the screen. I thought on that and noticed that the distance seems even more difficult to achieve with interior design projects than when designing buildings or objects. It is as if the envelope captivates one's creativity. It could be argued that the alliance established between the creator and his work is even more intense when it comes to interior design – the definition of the immediately perceptible layer of space that gives shelter to our daily activities. This is particularly significant as regards the domestic space and the intimate familiarity that characterizes this link when the client is, in turn, the future inhabitant of the house.

I also discovered that many of the authors of the works displayed here do not recognize the traditional boundaries between the different design disciplines: architecture, industrial design, interior design, urban planning, and graphic design. In fact, most of them are highly skilled architects and professionals with advanced degrees and many of them have been able to complete their ambitious training cycles with remarkable international experience. The democratization of higher education has led to a surplus of graduates who, either by vocation or by obligation, devote all their time, knowledge, and passion to interior design. Surely, this fact could explain part of the spectacular development and enrichment experienced by this discipline in recent decades. Decoration has traditionally been considered a superficial coating inevitably associated with variegated environments with profuse upholstery, whimsical prints, or heavy curtains. We can consider that traditional meaning fully overcome. Behind the best current interiors we discover authentic projects set out and solved using the same methodology and ambition as the architecture that shelters them.

Furthermore, the aforesaid dissolution of the academic and disciplinary boundaries is consistent with the gradual loss of cogency of the geographical boundaries. It is obvious that globalization and the universal and immediate access to information also involve obvious benefits, especially in a field in which the influence of environmental factors is not so relevant. In this regard, this works' selections also echo the keys that govern the new world order. The book contains projects from all latitudes, including some from emerging countries that assert the new role of these countries. A more significant presence of projects from the African continent would be desirable. Hopefully we will see a greater number of projects from that part of the world in the near future.

Beyond these modest considerations, this book constitutes a representative sample of the wonderful and exciting time in which domestic interior design stands and its contents invite us to be optimistic about the next evolution.

PREFACE

BY
JOÃO TIAGO AGUIAR

The world is changing. The economic recession, especially in Europe, has had an effect on architectural business in general. Where there were a thousand commissions to design and build something new, now there are almost none. Besides that, there are also too many empty buildings such as apartments, office buildings, housing blocks, and commercial units.

Therefore, architects have had to somehow reinvent themselves in order to survive in this critical period. In reaction to this general economic chaos, refurbishing started to make sense and gained a whole new importance. Refurbishment became, then, a very important part of the process. People don't have as much money anymore, banks don't loan money as easily anymore, and so what is left for the common citizens who can't afford to buy a new house? They refurbish their apartment. People try to improve their houses rather buy new ones and move. Nowadays, it is not so rare to have small commissions such as the refurbishment of a single kitchen or the bathrooms in a house. People improve or try to improve what they can afford to; it's as simple as that.

Architects have to adapt themselves to this new reality in order to survive. But not everything is as bad as it may sound! For instance, sometimes when you're designing something from scratch, it can take up to 5 or 6 years before you see it built. With refurbishing, things work out much faster. You design something and in a couple of months you see the final result. You can experiment with different solutions and in a short period see how it works. Things go much faster.

People may think an apartment or a little bathroom or a single kitchen is something simple but let us not mistakes ourselves: sometimes a little space is much more difficult to control and to make something nice out of than a big one. Everything has to be highly controlled in order to make sense and so it becomes a good project, and of course, satisfies the customer's initial program and needs.

Designers should always try to make the best out of anything that comes to them. No matter how small the project is, they must constantly treat it the same way: giving their best and respecting its individuality in order to make something unique and special.

Although times are tough at the moment, think positive. Keep faith that better times will come back soon. We will turn around! I say this not only because I believe in positive thinking, but also because I believe in the value of the individual person and his consciousness. I believe that the freedom and endless spontaneous creativity of individuals will allow us to turn around.

We have to believe in ourselves, in each other, and in people in general. I truly believe that positive thinking and trust can make a change. Architects and designers, please always keep in mind the romantic idea that when you're designing something, you have the power to transform the world into a better and more beautiful place.

CONTENTS

PHOTOGRAPHER: FERNANDO GUERRA / FG+SG

Apartment Rodrigo da Fonseca II

The project was to convert a dark basement with several interior compartments located on Rodrigo da Fonseca Avenue into a spacious and bright apartment.

Various walls were demolished and the entrance and distribution of the house were reorganized in order to transform the basement into a fluid and less compartmentalized space. At the back, the few small windows gave way to large windows that open up to the level of the deck.

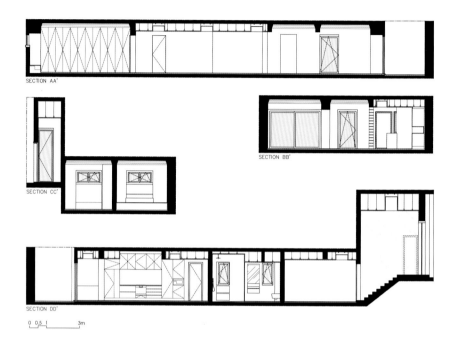

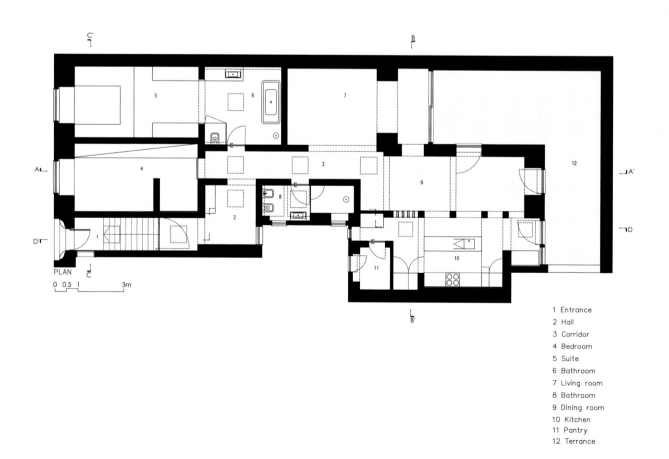

1 Entrance
2 Hall
3 Corridor
4 Bedroom
5 Suite
6 Bathroom
7 Living room
8 Bathroom
9 Dining room
10 Kitchen
11 Pantry
12 Terrance

APARTMENT RODRIGO DA FONSECA II LISBON, PORTUGAL | JOÃO TIAGO AGUIAR

1001

1001 is a minimalist home located in Tokyo, Japan.
It was designed by Keiji Ashizawa. 1001 is located in
Nakano City, one of Tokyo's 23 special wards. The
space is comparable to Ashizawa's other projects,
which all have an industrial and darker complexion.
In this particular project, the ceilings are beautifully
exposed with semi-transparent partitions separating
the different rooms.

It's dark in tone and dramatic in application, but also
features light that filters in through windows, pops
of color, and a grounded sense of calm and energy.
Gunmetal grays, blacks, and deep navy blues make
the space rich, while details such as the double-sided
desk and its window make it fun.

PHOTOGRAPHER: KATE DEL FANTE SCOTT

House Aupiais

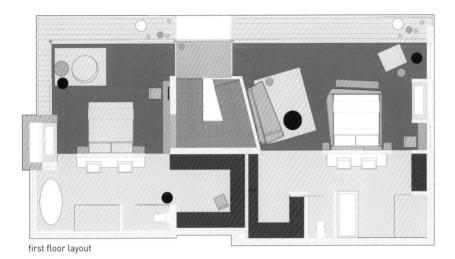

first floor layout

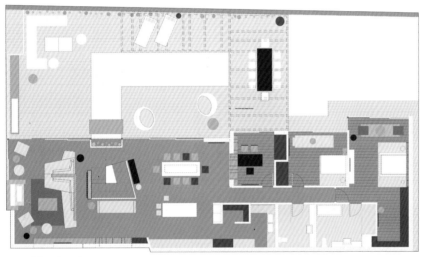

ground floor layout

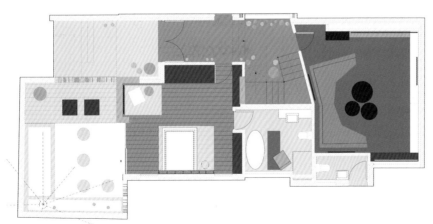

basement level layout

Site Interior Design was approached by a couple to finish the shell of their newly purchased, though technically incomplete, Camps Bay home. The house was a contemporary shell but needed a finishing layer to make it a home.

From the outset, the clients were open-minded and came with an exciting frame of reference and good aesthetic sensibilities. Contrary to the default bleached beach house aesthetic so prevalent in the area, a rich palette was realized with natural materials bringing warmth and highlights to the resulting dramatic rooms.

The spaces were furnished with a balanced combination of well-known local and international furnishing brands in combination with a substantial number of custom-designed and manufactured feature pieces. The goal was to create a diverse series of striking environments, each unique, but with a recognizable design DNA connecting them as a family of patently related spaces.

The bedrooms were finished in varying neutral tones. Furniture was selected or designed specially to live alongside bespoke headboards, bed bases, and natural, woven designer rugs and throws. Quirky objects and iconic lamps come together to add a sense of individuality to each of the rooms. The cavernous basement space is transformed into the ideal entertainer's retreat affectionately called the Legend Room by the owners. The reflective surfaces contrast with the matte walls and the unusual wetsuit fabric of the custom-designed sofa especially shaped to fit the unusual wall configuration of the existing structure. The materials used throughout the home set the base palette, but are designed to be interactive and intended to be curated by the owners, encouraging them to accumulate art pieces and exhibit them in various often changing configurations. The incorporation of sustainably sourced timber paired with luxurious linens and worn leather upholstery tempers the otherwise warm, dark interiors.

Each element of the house is intended to be an opportunity to build upon the theme of neutrals and naturals set off against contrasting materials and colors. All work together to create a striking visual impact; the final result is a bold, livable interior with a clear identity.

House Aupiais' interior was designed by Nina Sierra Rubia and Greg Scott.

Bangkok Flat

This project is a renovation of an apartment unit in an old residential high-rise in Bangkok. The design made use of as many existing attributes and found conditions as possible. The building's location, while in the middle of the city, is away from main roads and near one of Bangkok's largest waterways, or 'klongs.' The apartment itself is located at one corner of the high-rise. In Bangkok, prevailing winds originate from the south-west direction, and as a result, the layout was arranged to maximize openings to the east and south sides to allow for cross ventilation. Upon entering the apartment, one faces an uninterrupted view of the Bangkok skyline.

Materials and finishes were selected to create a contemporary interpretation of Thai living. In particular, inspiration was found during visits to local workshops of craftsmen and carpenters. These workshops usually consist of not only their work areas, but also combine eating and sleeping areas within a limited space.

The idea of combining several functions within a compact space resulted in the design of the outdoor shower area. Working closely with a local carpenter who used wood scavenged from demolished buildings and structures, perforated wooden screens were designed using reclaimed hardwood timber. When not used as a shower, these wooden screens can be closed to enlarge the outdoor balcony space.

PHOTOGRAPHER: ALLARD VAN DER HOEK

Weteringschans

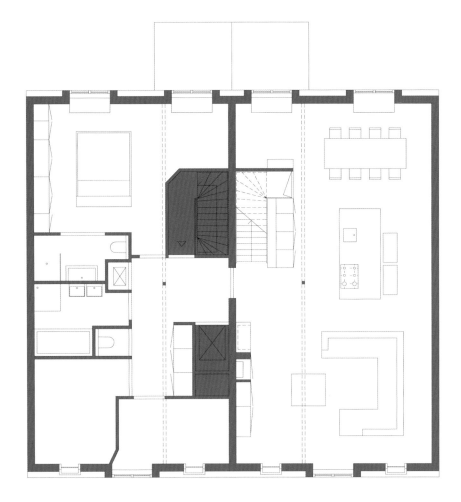

1. Living Room
2. Kitchen
3. Dining Room
4. Master Bedroom
5. Ensuite Bathroom
6. Bathroom
7. Bedroom
8. Bedroom
9. Hallway
10. To roof terrace

Located in the center of Amsterdam, this 160 m² 4th floor apartment is accessible directly from the elevator. This apartment is the result of merging two adjacent apartments. The emergency staircase was hidden in a kitchen so that the area of the original entrance hall of one apartment could be included. One half of the apartment has been designed as a loft. The big living and dining areas are informally separated by two kitchen units in the heart of the loft. We used a dark walnut veneer for the units that contrasts with the light interior. The large white cabinet is the brother of the high kitchen cabinet and serves as a bookcase, TV cabinet, storage, and central heating. The adjustable LED lighting is integrated into the existing beam construction and strengthens the ceiling lines. Through the minimalist intervention, the loft with its original beam pattern becomes a serene, spacious, and light space.

The other half of the apartment features a spacious lobby with lift access, several bedrooms, and a bathroom. The master bedroom has a private ensuite bathroom in a niche. The bathroom was inspired by a cave, which is reflected in the black mosaic accompanied by white casamood vetro tiles and zuchetti taps and shower fittings. The detached bed is the fourth element in the house and has a dark walnut finish. The stairs behind the kitchen give access to the roof terrace, which is 80 m² . The roof is realized in a single material and includes a lounge sofa and outdoor kitchen.

Skate Park House

This house is located in a quiet residential neighborhood in Shibuya ward. The owners, a young married couple, made a special request in regards to the design of their home. They wanted both a skateboard park and a piano rehearsal room to reflect their individual interests.

There was no need for a car park on the site, so to take advantage of the space, a private entrance courtyard was designed. The sliding glass panels of the first floor open up onto this enclosed area and allow for the workshop and studio to expand outwards. The studio has a skateboard bowl imbedded into the floor with multiple angles for plenty of different interaction.

The main living and dining space utilizes a similar concept of half-level changes to both separate and combine programs across the second story. Ceiling height differences and differences in material emphasize and create the boundary for the rooms. The presence of light throughout the residence serves to further connect the spaces. The top level is an all-private master suite. In order to create a break from the lower levels, the scale of the materials was increased. The overlapping layers of the floorboards create an ambiguous break between the rooms. The balcony, imagined as an interior garden, is not seen as a transitional space, but more a space for pause. It is the area most disconnected from the rest of the suite in terms of materials, and so is treated as the resting spot of the top floor.

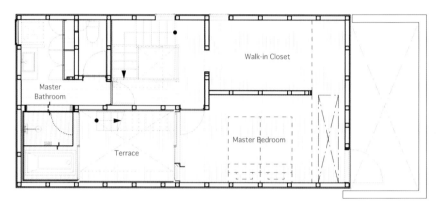

3F PLAN S=1:100

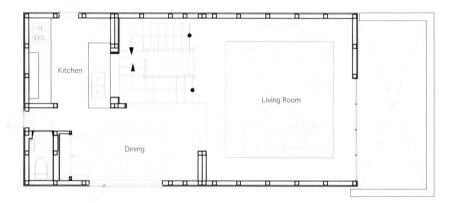

2F PLAN S=1:100

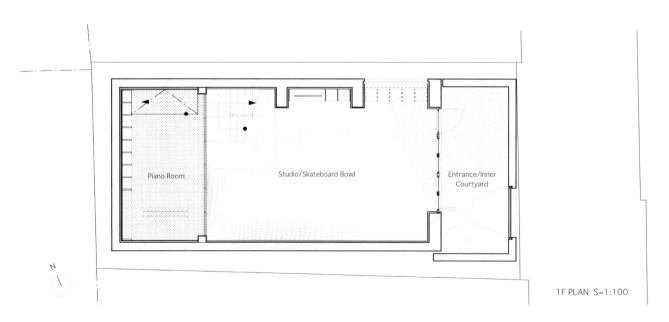

1F PLAN S=1:100

Home 06

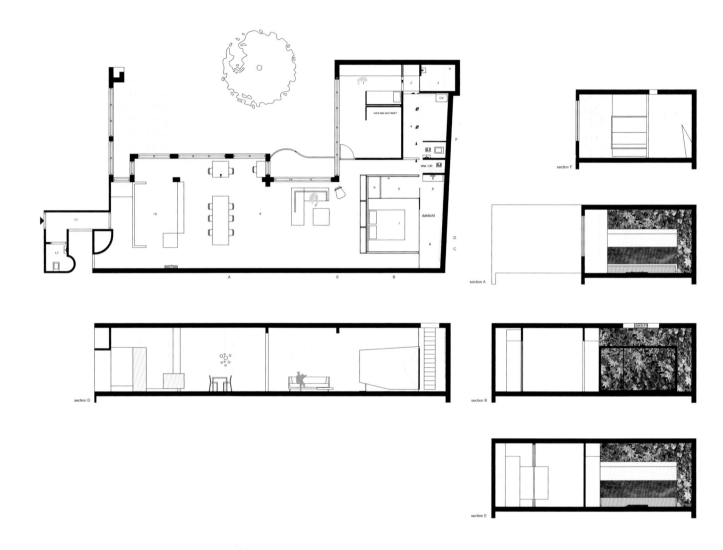

This residence at the Singel in Amsterdam, NL consists in a single open space in which the freestanding objects serve several purposes. The kitchen and wardrobe were placed near the entrance and combined into a single volume.

The bathroom and bedroom were combined into a volume at the back of the house. The open living area provides a view of the vertical garden and stairs to the roof terrace. The view of the green wall holds a promise that is redeemed once you enter the bed/bathroom. The small measurements of this combined bed and bathroom stand in contrast to its spaciousness. However, the room maintains a private and personal feeling.

The vertical garden and minimalist white bedroom create an intense contrast. Integration of nature is an important aspect of traditional culture in Japan, the homeland of the client. The integrated in-house vertical garden is an example of this. Other features include simplicity and minimalist details.

Home 07

This single-family apartment for four is situated in a stately building in southern Amsterdam, NL. The original structure, with rooms for staff, a double hall, and long hallways with lots of doors has been transformed into a spacious, transparent dwelling full of light and air.

The kitchen features white floor-to-ceiling cabinets with laser cut panels. This pattern results in a dynamic mixture of open and closed cabinets. The holes also function as integrated handgrips. The transparency of the object's skin gives depth to the volume, which is complimented by furniture like the Chair One by Grcic. An atrium with open staircases brings natural light from a large skylight into the living area.

A clear pine wall runs along the open staircase and connects the two levels. Upstairs the master bedroom is situated next to a large bathroom with a finish of structured tiles from Patricia Urquola, glass, and wooden cabinets.

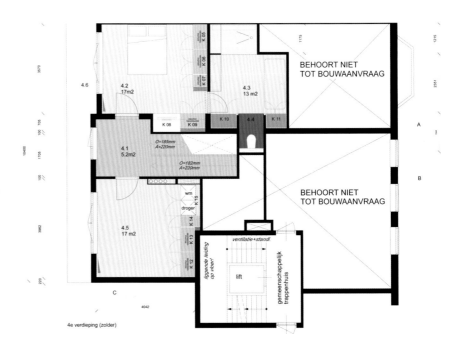

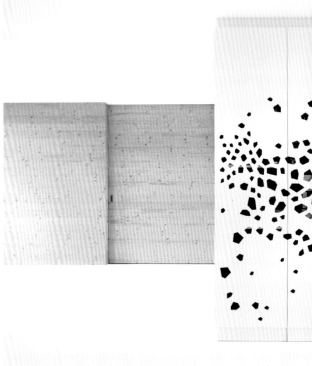

Home 08

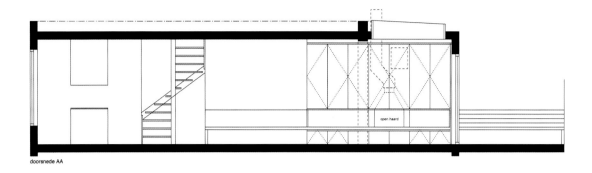

doorsnede AA

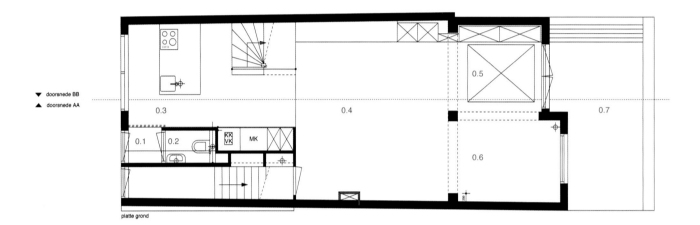

▼ doorsnede BB
▲ doorsnede AA

0.3

0.1   0.2   KR VK   MK

0.4

0.5

0.6

0.7

platte grond

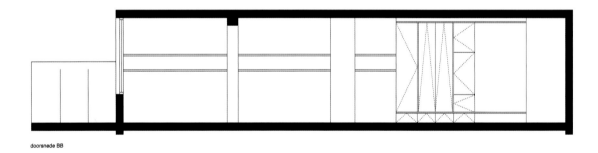

doorsnede BB

0.1 hal
0.2 toilet
0.3 keuken
0.4 woonkamer
0.5 aanbouw
0.6 zitkamer
0.7 buitenruimte

This small apartment in Amsterdam, NL (45 m²) was completely renovated because its foundation needed to be repaired. In its new layout, all the functions of the house are located in two wall units. The entrance hall, wardrobe, and kitchen equipment are hidden behind a pinewood wall. Opposite that wall is a second wall of the same material. The second wall integrates a bench, a fireplace, and storage. The floor, ceiling, and walls are all white. The fireplace as well as the custom-designed table and bench are anthracite gray. The simplicity of the design and choice of materials give this apartment lots of space despite the limited area.

RF Apartment

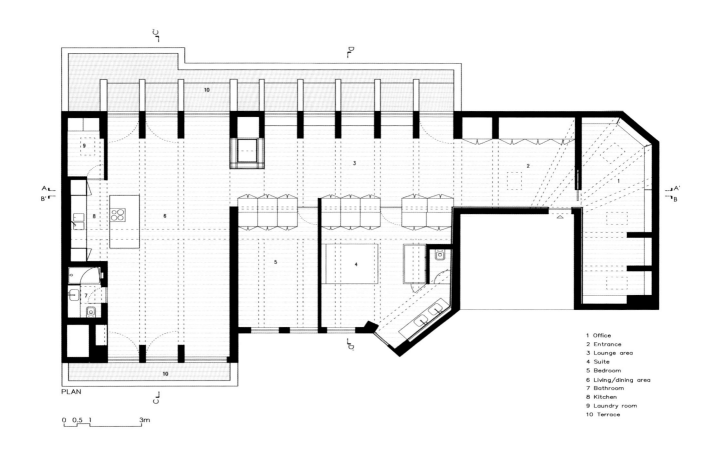

PLAN

0 0.5 1   3m

1 Office
2 Entrance
3 Lounge area
4 Suite
5 Bedroom
6 Living/dining area
7 Bathroom
8 Kitchen
9 Laundry room
10 Terrace

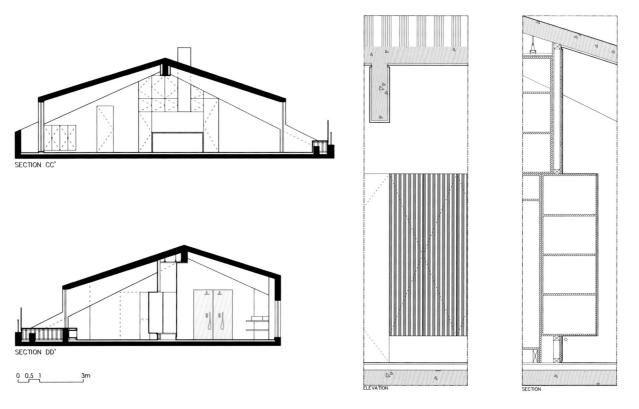

SECTION CC'

SECTION DD'

0 0.5 1   3m

ELEVATION

SECTION

The project was to transform an old office into an apartment. Situated on the top floor of a building in Avenida Rodrigo da Fonseca, the original space was uninteresting, had very little light, and was punctuated only by small openings at the top of the walls. The entire interior was demolished, leaving only the structural elements.

The small openings gave way to large windows that open onto the deck. The deck forms a balcony that surrounds the apartment. The space is fluid and less compartmentalized. A plan of bicolor cabinets animates the scene and separates the sleeping and living areas.

PHOTOGRAPHER: YUTA YAMADA, FUJISHOKAI

Omihachiman House

1st fioor

1: parking 2: approach 3: entrance 4: kitchen 5: dining 6: Japanese room 7: living room 8: wash room

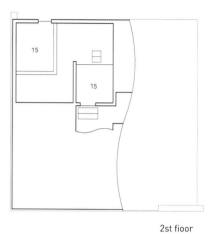

2st fioor

15:loft

3st floor

9: closet 10: study room 11: bedroom 12: void 13: children's room 14: balcony

Because the original house was very old fashioned, the designers reimagined the space in a modern way for this project.

The design connects each area with stairwells and small apertures so that it divides the space into small parts while connecting them. Meanwhile, each family member has their own place, but can look out over the spaces in the rest of the house.

Despite the small area, there is always a sense of space. The house feels simultaneously spacious and small. This ambiguity is the reason this house makes you comfortable.

House in Belas

The design is intended to project a contemporary look onto the main aspects of traditional Portuguese architecture. Special attention was paid to the balance and harmony between each building. The house consists of five different bodies linked through passages. The spaces between each body create a series of relationships; distances and views are generated, providing a rich and diverse atmosphere. The social areas are located in the core of the configuration and thus benefit from the surrounding environment. This design allows a simple and functional distribution throughout the house.

PHOTOGRAPHER: FRANCISCO NOGUEIRA

Lapa Apartment

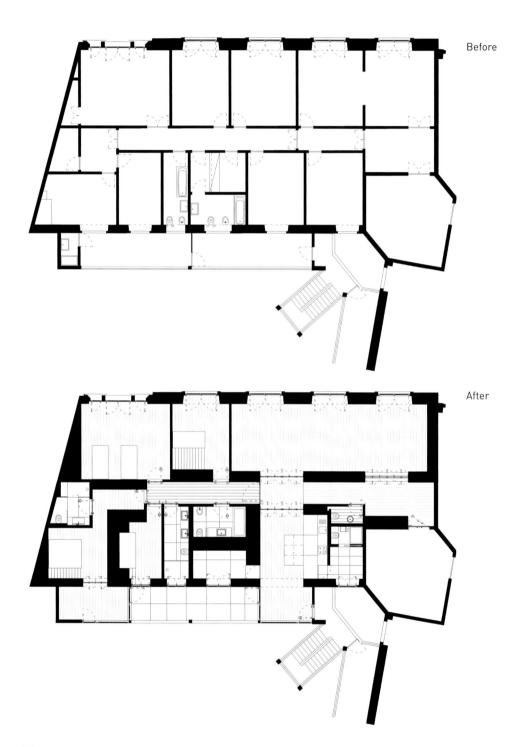

Before

After

This project was the complete refurbishment of an apartment on the 2nd floor of a building built in the first half of the twentieth century in Lapa, Lisbon. The original apartment was a good example of a layout common in Lisbon during that period: all the rooms were located off a central corridor that had no sources of natural light. The kitchen, located opposite the main entrance, led to an enclosed balcony used as a laundry room that connected to a service area with direct access from the building's second staircase. The plans were redesigned, creating and adapting the existing space into a contemporary living space. The long dark corridor was intersected in the middle, dividing the apartment into two main areas: social and private. The kitchen is now located in the center, and the direct connection to the living room provides the corridor with natural sunlight and unites both façades. The social areas can be closed independently by three sets of door panels that pivot to create different relationships and interactions depending on their position. Four bedrooms, one office, and three bathrooms were designed on the other half of the apartment. Thus, the design accomplishes its main goal: the transformation of the apartment into a contemporary and functional living space.

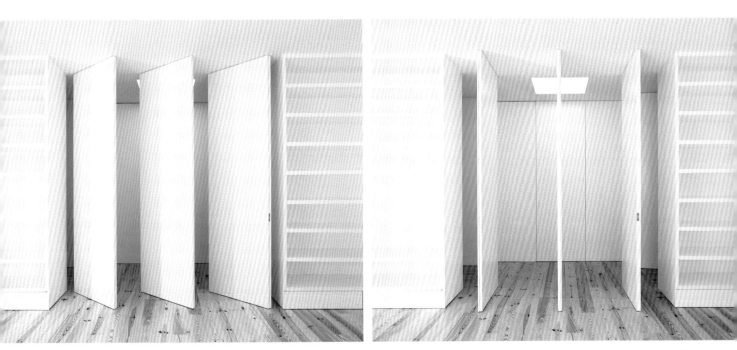

PHOTOGRAPHER: TOMAZ GREGORIC, JAN CELEDA

Level Apartment

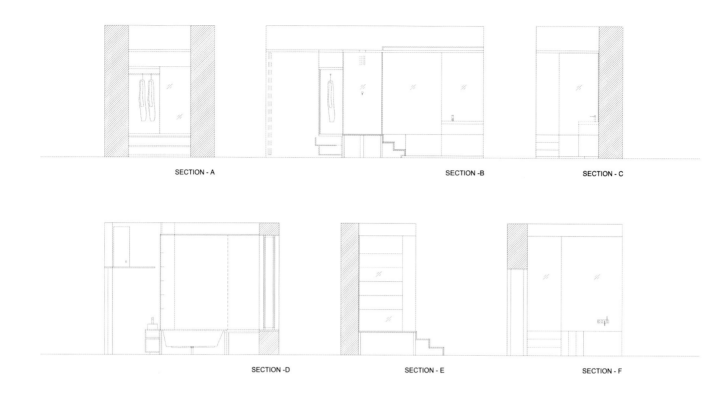

SECTION - A   SECTION -B   SECTION - C

SECTION -D   SECTION - E   SECTION - F

0   1   2m

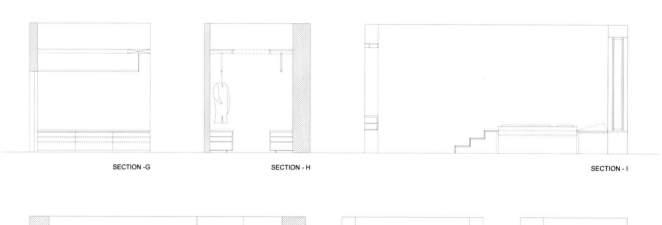

SECTION -G   SECTION - H   SECTION - I

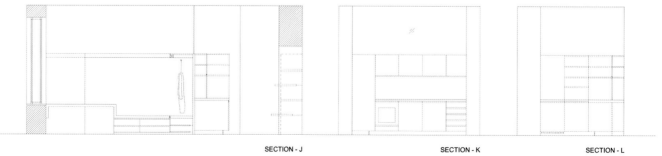

SECTION - J   SECTION - K   SECTION - L

0   1   2m

This project was the renovation of an apartment contained within a 1902 Art Nouveau building by architect C.M. Koch. The building is a 5 floor residential block in the center of Ljubljana, overlooking an adjacent square in a district that has residential and mixed use buildings.

The brief required an open layout with clearly defined spaces. The project features an open arrangement defined by rooms elevated to various heights. The elevated floors create an uninterrupted flow within the space. The space under the elevated floors is used for storage.

Retaining only the dominant structural partitions, the openness of the space creates a sense of unity. All the historical elements, such as doors and windows, were refurbished. The new materials are oiled and brushed oak, transparent or tainted glass, and white painted wood.

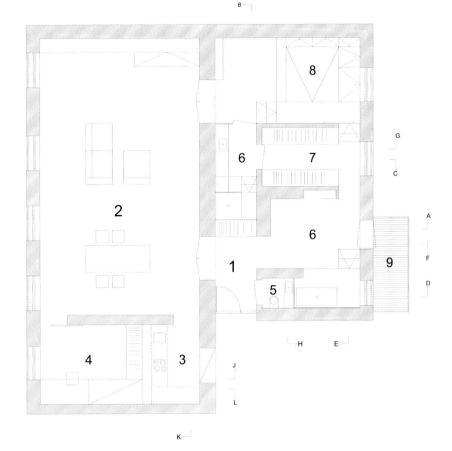

LEGEND

1 Entrance
2 Living room
3 Kitchen
4 Studio
5 Toilet
6 Bathroom
7 Wardrobe
8 Bedroom
9 Balcony

0   2.5   5m

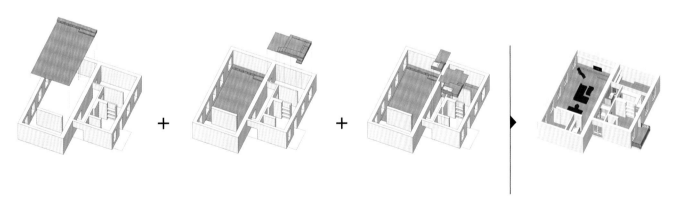

LEVEL 1: living room   LEVEL 2: bedroom   LEVEL 3: bathrooms

PHOTOGRAPHER: FERNANDO GUERRA / FG+SG

Apartment Bairro das Colónias II

The apartment, located in a building from the late '40s, had a good spatial distribution that the existing circulation spaces only exaggerated. Thus, the designers opted to keep the original spatial structure and joined the circulation areas to the living spaces in order to make the central and social areas more spacious.

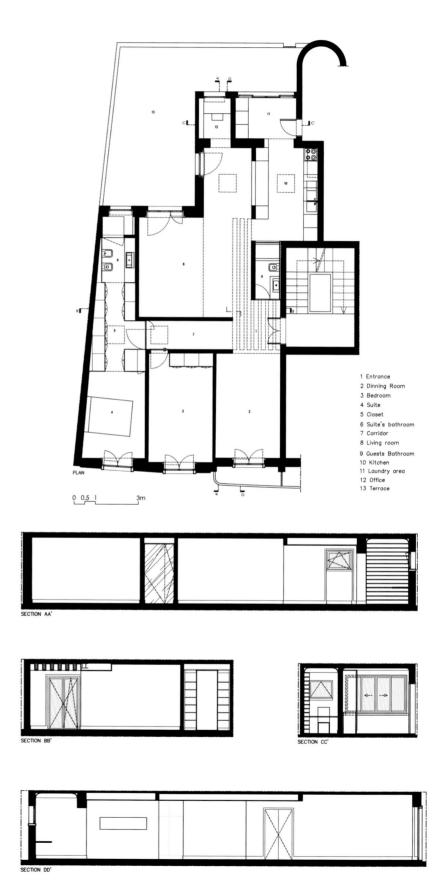

PLAN

0 0.5 1   3m

1 Entrance
2 Dinning Room
3 Bedroom
4 Suite
5 Closet
6 Suite's bathroom
7 Corridor
8 Living room
9 Guests Bathroom
10 Kitchen
11 Laundry area
12 Office
13 Terrace

SECTION AA'

SECTION BB'   SECTION CC'

SECTION DD'

APARTAMENTO BAIRRO DAS COLÓNIAS II LISBON, PORTUGAL | JOÃO TIAGO AGUIAR

Casamanda

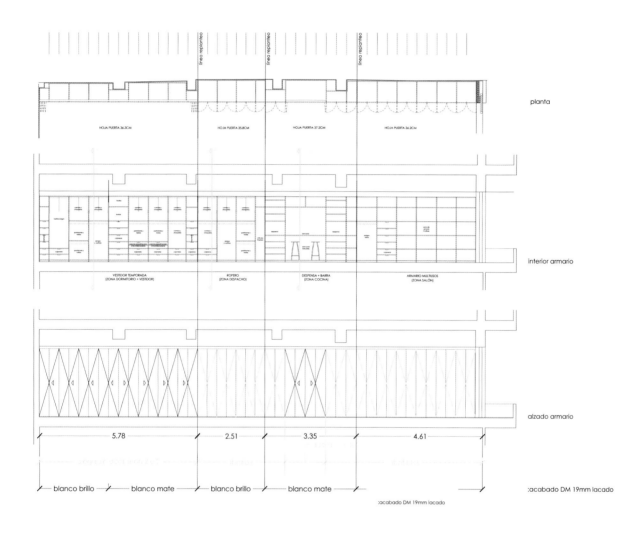

planta

HOJA PUERTA 36.3CM   HOJA PUERTA 35.8CM   HOJA PUERTA 37.2CM   HOJA PUERTA 36.3CM

interior armario

VESTIDOR TEMPORADA
(ZONA DORMITORIO + VESTIDOR)   ROPERO
(ZONA DESPACHO)   DESPENSA + BARRA
(ZONA COCINA)   ARMARIO MULTIUSOS
(ZONA SALÓN)

alzado armario

5.78   2.51   3.35   4.61

blanco brillo — blanco mate — blanco brillo — blanco mate   :acabado DM 19mm lacado

:acabado DM 19mm lacado

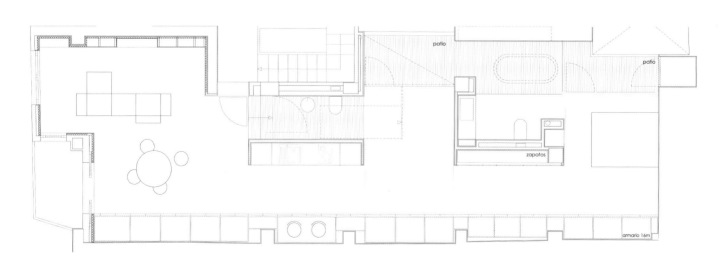

patio   patio

zapatos

armario 16m

We all have a passion, and the client's is her shoe collection. The collection contains one hundred and fifty pairs. This passion helped form a project loaded with functionality and appeal.

This project redefines the concept of the dividing wall. The wall was turned into a storage band that houses a whole personal universe. This band goes all across the dwelling, characterizing a number of rooms including the hall, living room, kitchen, study, and bedroom.

The layout, which was originally highly compartmentalized, is now void and thus creates a visual and spatial continuity that allows the light coming from the main façade and the two patios to reach most of the rooms. Only the service rooms stay more private.

Finally, the use of neutral colors in the finishes, only interrupted by the color of the client's personal belongings and furniture, will turn this dwelling into a unique space.

33M

Elenberg Fraser's new residential project, perfectly positioned at the edge of Melbourne's CBD, creates a vertical village that follows a story of ascendance and transcendence, inspired by the ancient myths of the angel Metatron (or Enoch, or Elijah) and Pandora's Box.

This project's massing is crucial to its design. Broken into a series of six white concrete towers of varying heights, and bound by a central lift core, 33M's profile mirrors Melbourne's skyline, creating a city within a city – a juxtaposed silhouette of its geographic context.

The buildings are clad in Metatron's feathers. At the lower levels, the loose feathers wrap around all four sides of the podium, forming a sunshade around the bronze glass. The upper levels of the tower are abutted with white concrete panels that also feature feather-like forms, giving them nap and grain.

There are four rooftop garden areas, designed in collaboration with Oculus, which have garden walls, sun lounges, and a pool. As you enter the lobby, you open Pandora's box and ascendance shifts to transcendence, as infinite mirrors create the sensation of a body suspended in space. It looks like a cracked open box and the patterned light forms a path through the black depths. The apartments themselves are filled with light. Their sliding doors enable the space to be reconfigured so that residents can choose whether to integrate the front room into living environments.

33M gives you the bird's-eye perspective and convenience of the inner-city high-rise lifestyle with the amenities of a house or large complex. The sky really is the limit here!

Level 4 floor plan

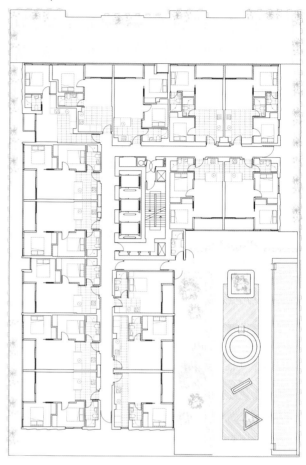

Level 4 floor plan

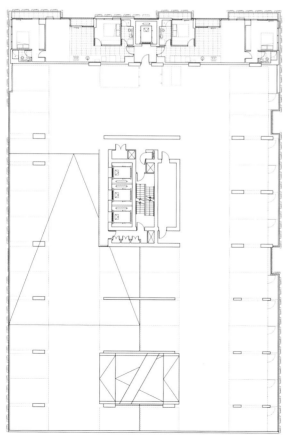

Typival apartment floor plan

33 MACKENZIE STREET

TREET

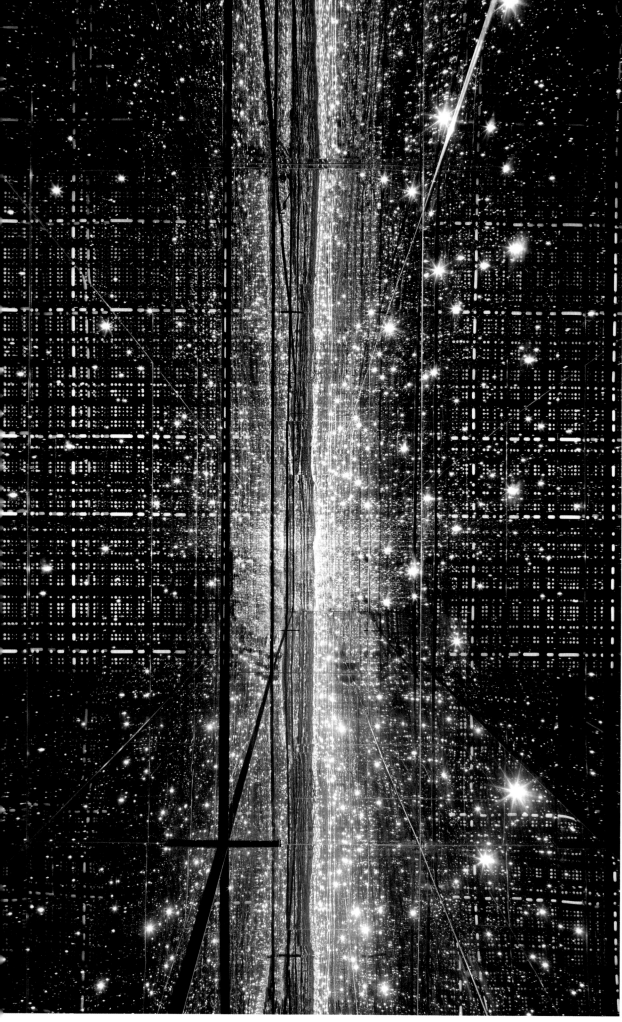

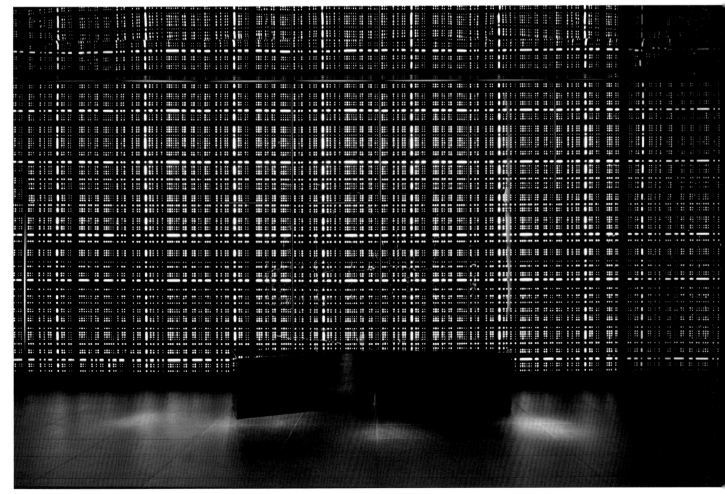

PHOTOGRAPHER: FAUSTO MAZZA

Apt. Av Monte Carlo MC

APPARTAMENTO IN MONTECARLO
PIANTA PIANO PRIMO

1 CAMERA
2 CAMERA
3 BAGNO
4 CAMERA
5 BAGNO

APPARTAMENTO IN MONTECARLO
PIANTA PIANO SECONDO

6 GUARDAROBA
7 BAGNO
8 CAMERA
9 CAMERA
10 STIRERIA

APPARTAMENTO IN MONTECARLO
PIANTA PIANO TERZO

11 CUCINA
12 SOGGIORNO
13 BAGNO

APPARTAMENTO IN MONTECARLO
PIANTA PIANO SOPPALCO

14 SOGGIORNO
15 STUDIO
16 DEPOSITO

The project fused and radically restructured three existing apartments in an early 20th century building in the heart of Monte Carlo. First a new staircase was built. The designer decided to differentiate the first levels with a generational key. The first floor is devoted to the children. The second floor, which is more intimate and compact, is for the parents. The third floor is designed for living together and hospitality, and so contains the living room and kitchen. Finally, there is a loft space where the informal and compact space becomes a place of happy anarchy for relations and activities. The space is used as a joint study and leisure area. With this division of space, the designer has created a home with reverse vertical development. The entrance is at the top, on the third floor, housing the living room and loft. Descending we come to the most private areas: the second floor for the parents and youngest children, and the first floor for the older and more independent children. The first floor can be accessed from the condominium stairwell.

Two-Story Detached House

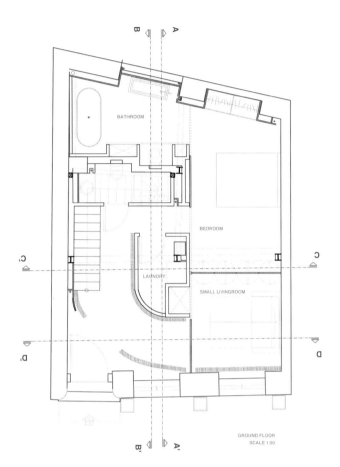

GROUND FLOOR
SCALE 1:50

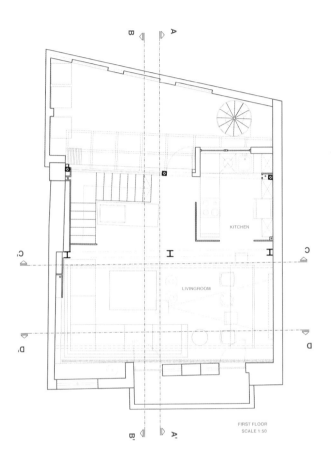

FIRST FLOOR
SCALE 1:50

The project was the reconstruction and reconfiguration of a postwar two-story detached house located in the area of Thisio in Athens.

Aside from the restoration work which had to be done for the statics of the building, the configuration of the spatial organization was another significant part of the project.

The interiors of detached houses built in the 1950s were typically designed with a ground floor intended for daytime functions that contained the living room, kitchen, and perhaps a small WC. The second floor was intended for nighttime functions and contained a storage and laundry room and a back balcony.

The aim of the project was to exploit the view of the Acropolis and to make it the most important element in the final spatial configuration.

The new design achieved that goal and inverted the interior of the house. The ground floor now houses the master bedroom as well as the master bathroom, a small living room that can be transformed into a guest house with the help of movable elements, a storeroom, and a small WC.

Because the ground floor only got light through the windows, the walls and doors have been removed and replaced with big movable panels.

Opposite the entrance, a staircase leads to the floor where a single space has been created. The space includes a living room, a dining room, and a kitchen that continues straight toward the veranda. A big glass wall was built to provide a view of the Acropolis. From the veranda, a steel stair leads to the terrace, which offers a superb view of Attic sky, the Acropolis, and the observatory.

Seatondale 01 – Heritage Interior

The project was to renovate a residence built 150 years ago. The heritage residence imposed restrictions on the designers. However, a design to suit a modern lifestyle was required. The historical residence filled the designers with curiosity. When the residence was built, people had a shorter average height, so why did the building have an excessive 4m ceiling height? Why was it necessary to have enormous 30cm timber skirting? From a modern perspective, the decorations around windows and doors could also be called excessive. Inside this residence there existed a world irrelevant to modern senses of scale and necessity.

The designers consolidated the lighting, storage, etc. into a 60cm thick box at the doorways of each room in order to accommodate a modern lifestyle. When looking from the corridor, it was as though nothing had changed since the house was built. The original fireplaces, timber skirting, and decorations at windows and doors came into view, making it look like the residence had remained unchanged. However, if you step through a doorway, and then turn to face it, you will see the minimal, modern White Box. The White Box is equipped with up lighting to highlight the excessive height of the ceiling. This minimal design brings the original decorative design to life. By respecting the existing elements and incorporating the excessive original decorations into a modern lifestyle, the designers discovered the historical importance of design. Furthermore, through the subtle contrast between the existing design and the additional design, the designers found their answer to the coexistence of historical and modern designs.

PHOTOGRAPHER: KIYOTOSHI TAKASHIMA

K Residence Renovation

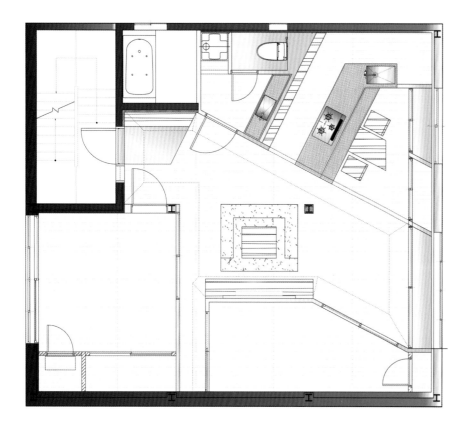

This project was a renovation project for a private flat in a reinforced concrete building. The owner wanted to have two private rooms, a space where friends could gather, and to incorporate greenery. The designer looked at the space with communication in mind and formed a design intended to connect the space with people and greenery. The designer wanted to create a space similar to a labyrinth in which you could lose your sense of direction.

The designer created walls of varying heights to create a series of interesting connections throughout the apartment. These connections, coupled with the structure of the private rooms, created the desired labyrinth effect. In order to create a strong connection with greenery, the designer created a wall that will eventually be totally covered with foliage.

The designer applied frosted glass to the south wall to allow sufficient light to enter the space and maintain privacy. Adjustable boxes were arranged in the communication space. The boxes can be used as backrests, chests, tables, etc. This interactive feature offers its users a further chance to connect with each other. The designer applied mortar to the kitchen and other utilities to contrast with the organic wood and plants. The designer also used mortar for the pillar to give the space a feeling of objectivity. The pillar supports the physical structure of the home and gives the space stability .

Residence Liu

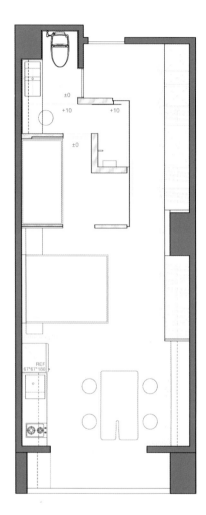 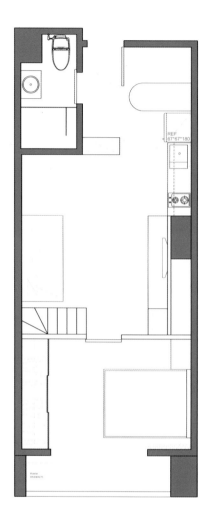 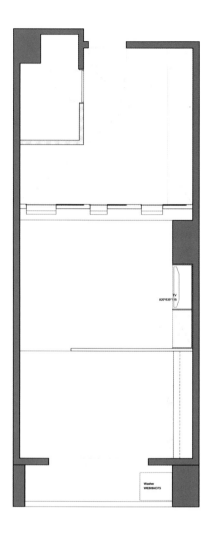

The designers made the child's bedroom the center of the long and narrow space. The design helps to facilitate interaction between the parents and their child.

In Taiwan, it is customary to place the crib near the parents' bed. This design offers an alternative that makes the child's bedroom the core of the space, but affords the parents more privacy. The child's bedroom features movable elements that allow it to be either connected with or closed off from the surrounding space.

The master bedroom is separated from the kitchen by a curtain to ensure privacy. All the storage is located along a long wall to maximize space.

For the loft the designers incorporated a wall with open doors that serve three different functions. First, they allow the child to climb around and see between the bedroom and the loft. Second, they enable the parents to easily attend to their child's needs. Third, they improve airflow and increase the amount of natural light in the interior.

Optical Glass House

This house is located among tall buildings in downtown Hiroshima, overlooking a busy street. In order to create a private and tranquil environment, the designer placed a garden and glass façade on the street side of the house. The garden is visible from all the rooms in the house, and the serene, soundless scenery of the passing cars and trams imparts a richness to life in the house. Sunlight from the east refracts through the glass and creates beautiful patterns on the floor and walls. The rain that hits the skylight creates patterns on the entrance floor. Light filters through the trees in the garden and lands on the living room floor. A super lightweight metal-coated curtain dances in the wind. Although the house is located downtown, it enables the residents to be aware of the changing seasons and enjoy the varying light and moods of the city as the day goes by.

A façade of some 6,000 glass block (50mm x 235mm x 50mm) was used. The large glass blocks effectively shut out sound and enabled the creation of an open, clearly articulated garden that admits the city scenery. To create such a façade, glass casting was used to produce glass of extremely high transparency from borosilicate. The casting process was exceedingly difficult because it required slow cooling to remove residual stress from within the glass as well as high dimensional accuracy. The glass retained micro-level surface asperities. However, the designer actively welcomed this effect since it would produce unexpected optical illusions within the interior space.

The façade would have been too heavy to stand on its own without reinforcement, so the designer punctured the glass blocks and strung them on 75 stainless steel bolts suspended from the beam above the façade. The façade looks like a waterfall flowing downward, scattering light and filling the air with freshness. In order to protect the structure from lateral stress, the designer placed flat stainless steel bars (40mm x 4mm) at 10 centimeter intervals. This technique resulted in a 6mm sealing joint between the glass blocks.

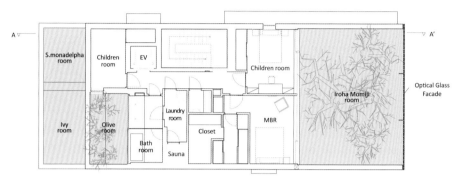

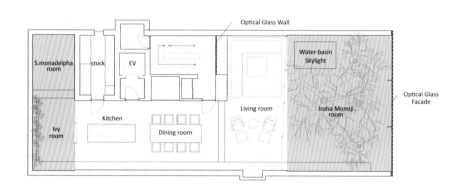

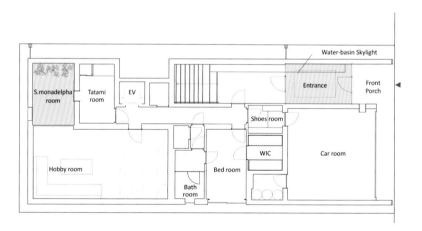

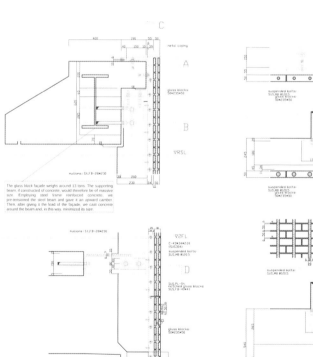

The glass block facade weighs around 13 tons. The supporting beam, if constructed of concrete, would therefore be of massive size. Employing steel frame reinforced concrete, we pre-tensioned the steel beam and gave it an upward camber. Then, after giving it the load of the facade, we cast concrete around the beam and, in this way, minimized its size.

facade section E

horizontal section A

horizontal section B

section C

horizontal section D

PHOTOGRAPHER: HIROYUKI OKI

M11 House

entrance

the second floor plan

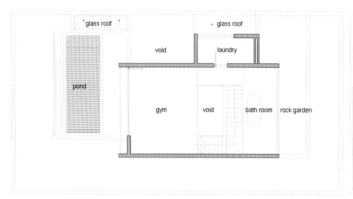

the third floor plan

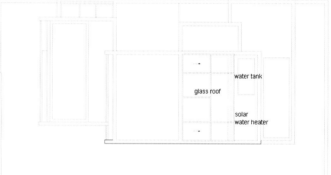

roof plan

M11 House is located in a suburban area in Ho Chi Minh City. The architect wanted to create an elegant and peaceful space where the client could escape the noisy and polluted environment of the developing city. In order to create such a retreat, the architect used natural materials such as wood and stone, utilized top lights, and placed small green courtyards inside the house.

In order to integrate nature into the design, the architect incorporated gardens into the home. The area where the largest tree is planted almost looks like another room. The sound of the rustling leaves resonates within the confined space.

The client admits that he was greatly influenced by the designers as they worked closely together on the project, meeting every weekend to share coffee and discuss progress. "I admired minimalism already, but Hiep (the designer) urged me far more strongly toward it. I also wanted to use a lot of steel. It's what was expected too because my year – the year I was born – is a metal year. Hiep guided me away from metal however, something most Vietnamese people would not allow." The client now concedes that the designer was right and that the wood fosters warmth throughout the home. However, there are, some concessions to his love of steel, including the Le Corbusier chair.

Wood is used extensively throughout the home, softening the concrete flooring and the colossal column that dominates at its core. Nose flute wood was chosen for its color and resistance to termites.

PHOTOGRAPHER: LORENZO CARONE

Fraciscio House

The height of the apartment allowed me to double the usable space. I built a wooden second skin that provides an interesting and uniform atmosphere. The house looks as though it was sculpted out of a block of wood, with the various rooms and furniture items emerging as a result of material subtraction. It exists without the need for walls. During the study and implementation of this project, special attention was given to the combination and treatment of materials. The entrance opens onto a larch wood living room that continues into the cooking corner. The living room area, left deliberately without interruptions, opens onto a second space that has a surprising and open arrangement. The door of the large wood cube leads to the night area where a central staircase separates the two bedrooms and leads to the upper floor. A transparent floor dilates an otherwise slightly suffocating space. The materials provide the architectural fabric for the apartment. The staircase is constructed from suspended planks of wood that look more like a sculpture than steps to be walked on. The extensive material uniformity creates a somewhat disorienting effect. This can be seen in the studio where it is hard to make out where things start and finish.

PHOTOGRAPHER: WALTER MAIR, B&Z

Musicians Apartment House

The various buildings of a disused factory dating from 1885 were transformed into a spacious home and work environment for musicians and their families. The building materials were not all good quality. The brick structures of the workshop and warehouse were adequate, and the buildings on lothringerstrasse, which once housed both the administrative offices and the factory floor, were used in the ensemble since they had a certain formal panache. Structures of minor architectural value were demolished and the remaining elements incorporated into the new development, forming an interesting conglomerate with special qualities.

Acoustic adaptations enable people to both teach and live in the new apartments. Guest apartments, training rooms, a sound/recording studio, a canteen, and a spacious children's play hall all form part of the new musicians' apartment house. The structural diversity of the original factory site meant that a separate conversion strategy had to be developed for each building. The former warehouse was the biggest building – a wooden structure with a spacing of 4 x 4 x 4 meters, surrounded by a massive external wall.

These characteristics have been integrated into and adapted to the new building; the internal wooden structure was copied onto the external wall with the use of concrete pillars and beams, and the diagonal steel supports also show the internal structure outside. The layout of the marionette apartments and flat shares mirrors the grid pattern of the old wooden structure. However, in one part the existing structure was weak and was therefore replaced with a new open courtyard living space.

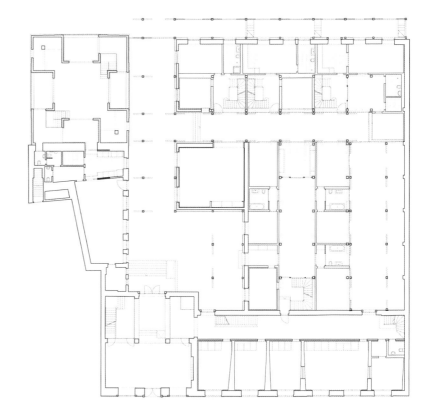

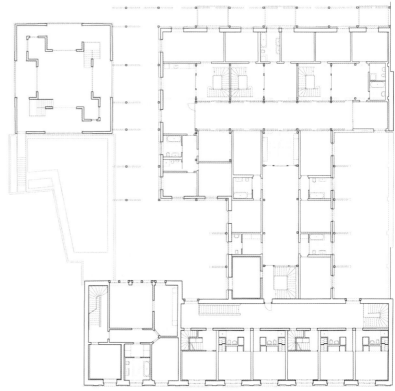

Kofunaki House

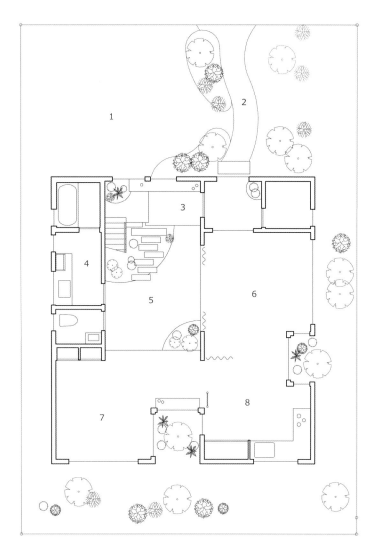

1st floor

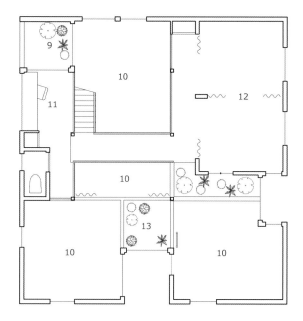

2st floor

People from ancient times loved to live with nature, especially the Japanese. They always enjoyed the changing of the seasons. Living with nature can be inconvenient and time and effort consuming. However, the natural light and plants make it worth the trouble.

Living with nature can be as healing as a smiling face and one can grow very attached to that way of life. Thus, the designers decided to incorporate nature into this design.

The inside and outside spaces of the home are gently connected to create an atmosphere where one can always feel close to nature and enjoy the seasons as they come and go.

This house has the power to soften a family's heart. The promise of a rich new life makes people enjoy the space and life.

PHOTOGRAPHER: FUMIHIKO IKEMOTO

House H

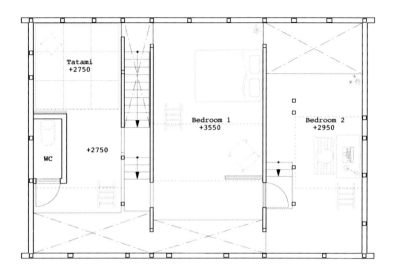

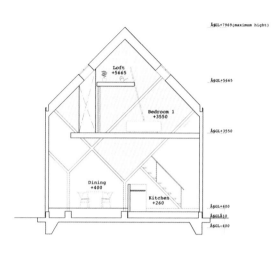

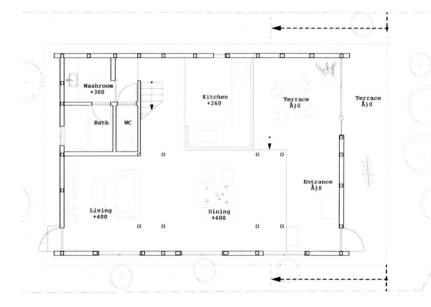

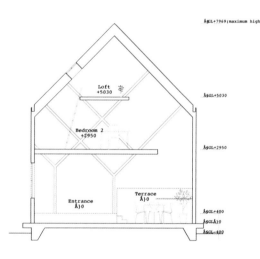

This is a house for a young couple and their child, located in Matsudo, Chiba Prefecture. Located on the outskirts of Tokyo, Matsudo City has developed primarily as a residential area since the 1960s. The project was to rebuild a house built during that period. The clients wanted the house to stand as a symbol for hope for the future.

The designer hoped to turn the house into a living symbol by creating a large roof and interior structure that would play an interactive role in the family's daily life.

The designer placed a big roof on the site and arranged Y-shaped wooden frames inside. The designer defined the space by hanging second floors and loft floors from the frames. The Y-shaped frames of bonded wood run throughout the entire house, like attic beams in traditional architecture. Six floorboards are hung from the frames at different levels. The distance from the roof and other living spaces vary depending on the level and location of the floorboards. The house is a single space under one roof, loosely divided by the Y-shaped frames and the floorboards.

The designer hopes that the family uses the structure of the house in their daily life, perhaps by hanging pictures from the frames or by marking the height of their child as he grows. In that way, their life will leave an imprint on the house.

MC Apartment Refurbishment

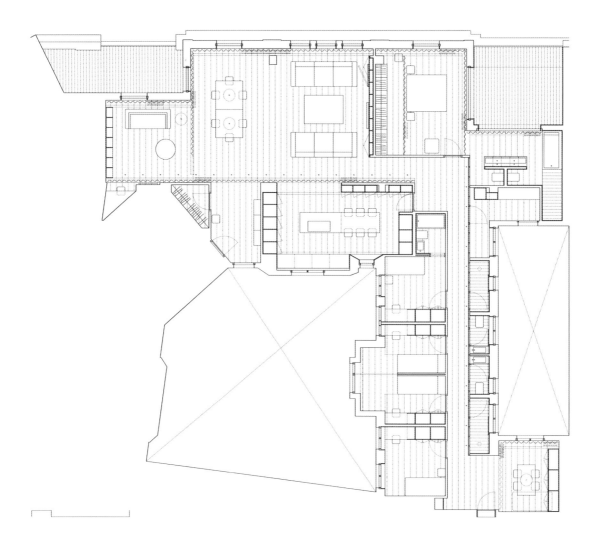

The original apartment was characteristic of the housing built during Pamplona's second expansion and was excessive and inappropriately distributed for current standards.

For the renovation of this apartment, modern living and aesthetics were taken into account. The walls are comprised of a curtain and perforated wood paneling. The walls and the repetition of similar elements give the areas throughout the home a uniform look and serene atmosphere. Net curtains and translucent glass were used to hide the façades in the kitchen and bathrooms. Perforated timber was used for the last layer of one of the courtyard façades to allow light to stream into the corridor and bathrooms. The discrete incorporation of the visible elements of the air conditioning system into the design is also worth noting. However, the most unusual element of the design is the use of curtains. The curtains serve to break down the boundaries of each space and give real character to the house.

Interior Design of Apartments in Serrano Street

Luxury, comfort, design, and quality have been joined in eight new flats in the center of Madrid. The newly renovated luxurious apartments were designed by A-cero. These apartments are the property of the Group VP Hotels and are located in an old four-story building. There are two apartments larger than 185 m² in each floor of the building.

Each apartment has a different layout, but each has the following rooms: four or more bedrooms with bathrooms, a kitchen, a lounge/dining room, a utilities area, and a toilette. The biggest apartments have servants' quarters. The large windows and skylights in the lounges, dining rooms, and halls allow a great deal of light to enter the flats. The white walls and roofs create an atmosphere of clarity, cleanliness, and warmth. All the flats have ample space and a functional distribution based on airy rooms and double height ceilings. The floors are made of travertine marble, wood, and dark gray porcelain tiles. A-cero designed the gray, black, and white furniture with clean and modern lines. The bathrooms and kitchens are fully equipped and were designed for maximum functionality. The decorative palette is largely neutral with splashes of red and yellow.

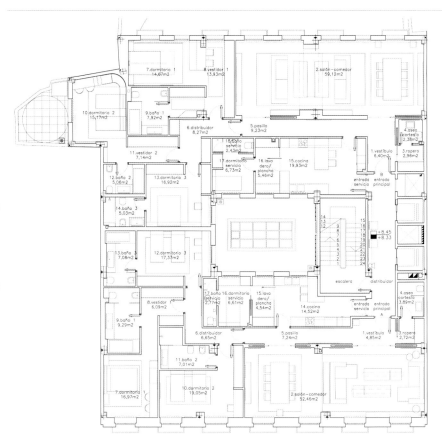

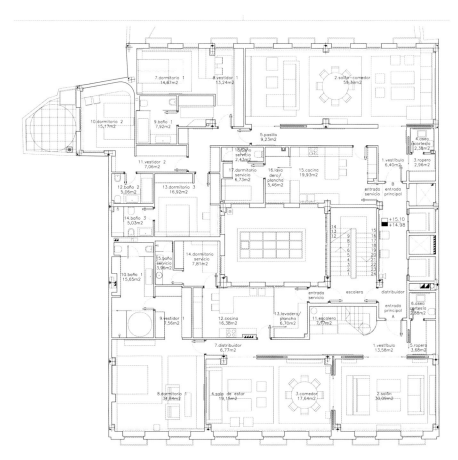

Porto Salvo

VIA PORTO SALVO

VIA PORTO SALVO

TERRACE

TERRACE

WARDROBE

MASTER
BEDROOM

RELAX

+2.85

LIVING

+2.55

STUDIO

TERRACE

DINING

+2.85

BEDROOM

KITCHEN

LAUNDRY

VIA BONER

VIA BONER

first floor plan

0   2   4m

second floor plan

0   2   4m

This building is one of the few that survived the earthquake of 1908 in Messina, Sicily. The project preserved most of the original elements including the marble stairs, the handmade floor tiles, the wood trusses, and the structural braces that reinforced the building after the earthquake. It is clear that the space is linked to a way of living from the past. Traditionally, houses and shops were often located in the same building and the long staircase that leads from the ground floor to the upper level is a remnant of that design. The main element of the interior space is the tall roof with its wood trusses. The new skylights flood the entire space with light. The recovery of the original roof greatly increased the amount of usable space in the interior, making it possible to add lofts. The space has a double height and contains several interactive elements including the entrance's long staircase, the living area, the dining area, the linear kitchen, and the gallery studio. The main bedroom has two different levels and the same exciting double height. The ground floor is an open space with a large walk-in closet and a bathroom with two wash basins and a large open shower.

The upper part overlooks the lower floor and houses the sleeping area. A second large bedroom is on a loft above the kitchen. From the living area and the kitchen you can access a 60 sqm terrace. The terrace is laid out on two levels and features a large counter that serves to extend the kitchen and break down the barriers between the interior and exterior spaces. The natural materials and soft color palette form a perfect dialog with the building's history. The white walls, plywood furniture, hand planed parquet floor, white metal stairs, and gray resin surfaces create a relaxing atmosphere within the 180 sqm of this house.

Apartment Penthouse Berlin

As a result of a competition, Lecarolimited was commissioned to remodel a penthouse in a German apartment building. The penthouse was spread over two floors and situated on a small but active street in the middle of a large gallery district. After studying the large apartment with its maze of partitions and closed off rooms, the designers proposed to introduce an element that would gently shape and define each space without closing it off. The principle ambition was to connect each space and provide continuity to the entire apartment.

The designers tested a number of options and settled on a mirrored element that would wrap and unfold throughout the apartment. The designers infused the design with both a Loosian sensuality and the mystery and magic associated with mirrors. Both the material and spatial applications helped to create a dynamic and whimsical atmosphere. To create what the designers called the "mirror belt," custom painted bespoke glass was fixed to a wooden substrate. The material has a unique look that avoids the intensity of standard mirrors.

Grundriss / Floor plan

① Eingang / Entry
② Küche / Kitchen
③ Essen / Dining
④ Sitzen / Seating
⑤ Schwarzer Flur / Black Corridor
⑥ Gästezimmer I. / Guestroom I.
⑦ Gästezimmer II. / Guestroom II.

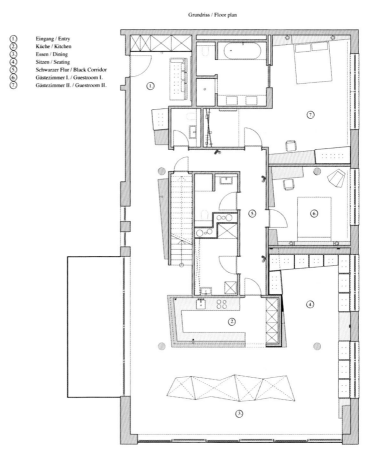

Grundriss Oben / Floor plan Top

⑧ Kamin & Bar / Chimney & Bar
⑨ Schlafzimmer / Masterbedroom
⑩ Arbeiten & Lesen / Work & Library
⑪ Dachterrasse / Roofgarden

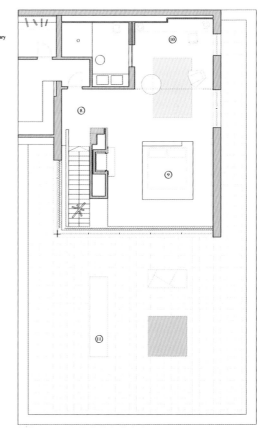

PHOTOGRAPHER: JOHN SHORT

The Rainbow House

The Rainbow House is a magical oasis on a busy street. When you step through its front door, you enter a parallel universe of fun, color, movement, and sensuality and leave the ordinary world far behind. The design concept for the Rainbow House was to create a living artwork filled with unique and magical elements. All the surprising and disparate elements are united by a central spiral staircase.

Visitors encounter the staircase as soon as they enter the double-height lobby from the street outside. The bespoke fiberglass and steel column passes through the entire color spectrum as it rises through the house. The staircase creates a visual rhythm felt throughout the house. Its colors emanate out and influence the color scheme on each floor. Sun pours down through skylights at the top of the house, drenching the staircase in light.

To maximize the amount of light in the interior, the designers removed every unnecessary wall, liberated windows, and added skylight after skylight. Light and energy bounce off luminous walls covered with super white polished plaster.

The designers left the outside nearly untouched, heightening the division between the noisy and hectic world outside and the magical world within. The one exception was the security grills, which can be seen through the windows from inside the house. They are knitted steel bars in ultramarine, creating a warm and happy security that hints at the personality of the house without allowing you inside.

PHOTOGRAPHER: AKINORI HAMADA, ALEX KNEZO

Barcode Room

Barcode Room is a concept studio apartment composed of walls that move freely from side to side. This feature allows the resident to customize the space to fit a variety of uses. The walls contain functional elements such as storage and furniture, which may be put away when not in use to maximize floor space. This design gives the inhabitant a comfortable space to live in that can be transformed into a great place to entertain guests.

Through the use of these walls, or bars, Barcode Room takes the typical studio space and allows it to be transformed into a space where one can live and friends can gather. Each wall is comprised of a combination of 12 types of components. Various types of bars (such as a living bar, kitchen bar, or sleeping bar) can be created by combining different components. These customizable bars allow the owner to create his own unique collection of layouts or barcodes.

Removing folded furniture from the walls creates windows that connect the spaces on either side of the walls. All the walls are on wheels and their movement is guided by a rail on the ceiling. This design makes it possible to install this versatile system in both new and existing apartments.

With continued development, we hope to create a product that will allow customers to freely change the space around them. Furthermore, if the size of the walls and the size and location of the components within the walls can be customized, customers will be able to redefine the spaces in which they live, play, and work on a daily basis. By developing a larger variety of components, the bars could also be used in a range of spaces including offices, galleries, stores, restaurants, etc.

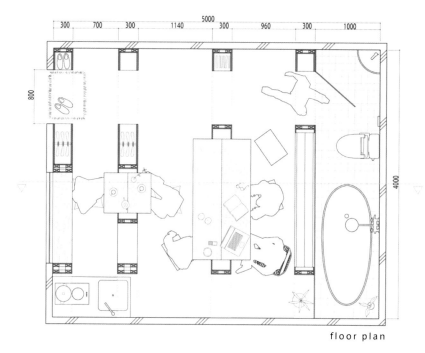

floor plan

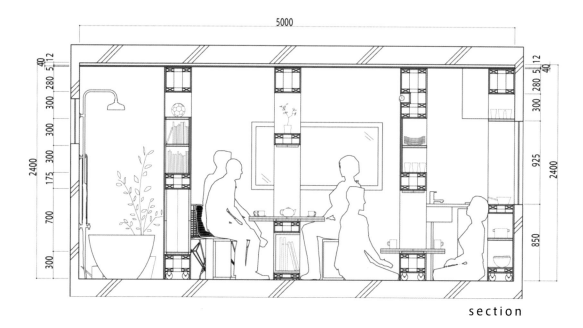

section

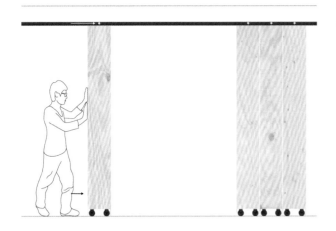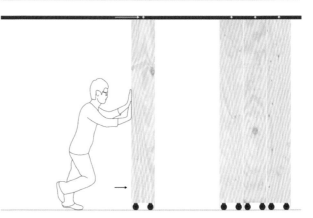

God's Loftstory

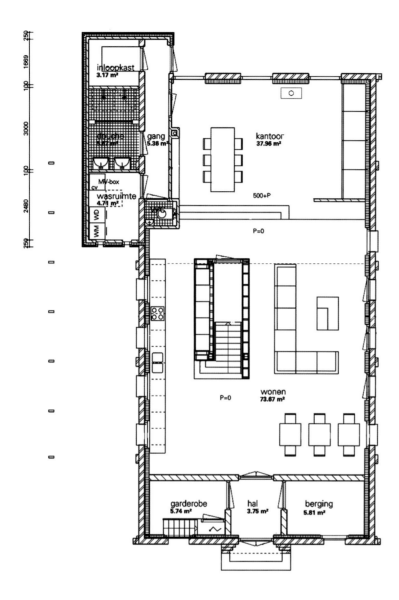

The old Dutch Reformed Evangelism Building in Haarlo was transformed into a unique loft. This project demonstrates that a transformation of a church with limited resources is possible if you use a smart design and an efficient plan. The concept was to strip, isolate, and furnish. The result represents the motto of the owners: "Cherish your inner child; remain pure, playful, explorative, and a little bit naughty!"

The designers purposefully chose not to fill the volume with as many rooms as possible in order to retain the spaciousness of the building. The only architectural additions are the mezzanine, which houses the relaxation room (couch, bed, and bath), and the multifunctional stairway. The stairway acts as a room divider, closet, kitchen, an acoustic element, and exhibition wall. All the new materials are pure, sober, functional, and inexpensive. Concrete was used for the floor, the original floorboards were used as cladding for the stairway, and stainless steel was used in the kitchen. A hard glass partition was used to retain openness, white stucco was used to brighten the interior. Strategically chosen red accents punctuate the otherwise neutral design.

The modern garden has large planters made from left over bricks. There is an herb garden, a vegetable garden, a flower garden, and an orchard. A 40ft shed was integrated into the wooden fence and equipped with a green roof.

This project reflects great passion, humor, respect, love, and creativity. It is exemplary because it achieved a great architectural transformation while conserving religious heritage.

Private House Madrid

The artistic sensibilities of the owners greatly influenced the design of this project. The main goal was to emphasize the owners' collection of artwork. Due to time constraints, the designers decided to focus on a single forceful element. They designed a central space that would open onto all the other rooms of the house. The space visually connects the entire house because it lacks barriers. Because it is the hub of the house, it is also an ideal place to display artwork.

The designers wanted to integrate this space with the rest of the house. They decided to use the roof to create spatial continuity throughout the dwelling.

The designers chose modern and neutral furniture that would not steal attention from the artwork. As a result, each finished space is itself reminiscent of a painting.

PHOTOGRAPHER: TORIMURA KOICHI, KOYAMA
SHUNICHI, TSUCHIDA TAKUYA

KRE

The most remarkable requests the client made were to have garage space for nine cars, to have his favorite car displayed in the living room, and to have a tall tree in the living room. In order to accommodate these requests, we designed a large building with an extensive basement.

The entire basement was utilized in order to create enough parking space. Then, a custom lift was made so that the client's Lamborghini could be moved from the basement to the living room floor. When the lift is lowered, a moveable floor slides into place to complete the living room floor. Instead of building another story, additional rooms were created from steel boxes, which we hung from the reinforced concrete structure. This design creates an attractive open space that can accommodate both the car and the tree.

The spaces under the boxes have undefined borders and each has a different function. The floating rooms make it possible to fit large items in the house and keep the living room open and spacious.

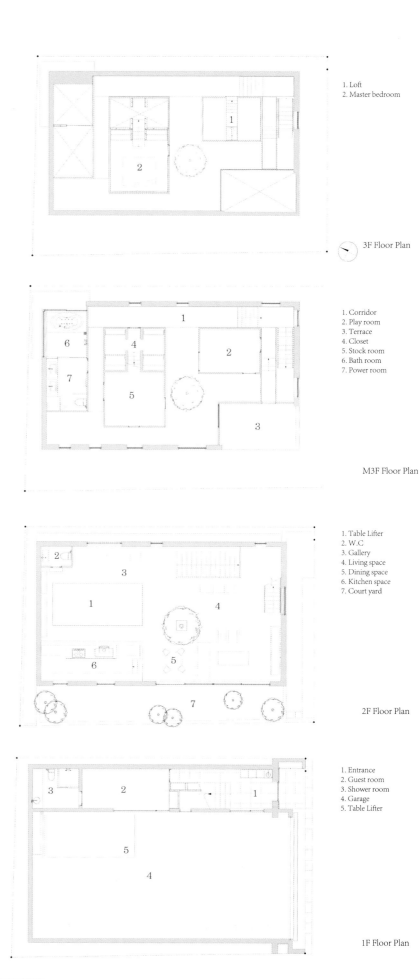

1. Loft
2. Master bedroom

3F Floor Plan

1. Corridor
2. Play room
3. Terrace
4. Closet
5. Stock room
6. Bath room
7. Power room

M3F Floor Plan

1. Table Lifter
2. W.C
3. Gallery
4. Living space
5. Dining space
6. Kitchen space
7. Court yard

2F Floor Plan

1. Entrance
2. Guest room
3. Shower room
4. Garage
5. Table Lifter

1F Floor Plan

PHOTOGRAPHER: ALAIN BRUGIER

Industrial Loft

This 100 square meter loft is located in the southern part of Sao Paulo and was designed for a bachelor. The project achieves a harmony between comfort and modernity and is industrial without feeling cold. In order to give the apartment uniformity, only one covering was used for the walls and ceiling. We chose burned cement for the main covering to create an atmosphere that was rustic and industrial yet warm and comfortable.

The lower floor is an open space that houses the living room, dining room, and kitchen. We chose to eliminate the barriers between the bedroom, bathroom, and closet in order to keep the mezzanine open and spacious.

Both the structure and ornamental elements of this apartment are completely contemporary.

House T

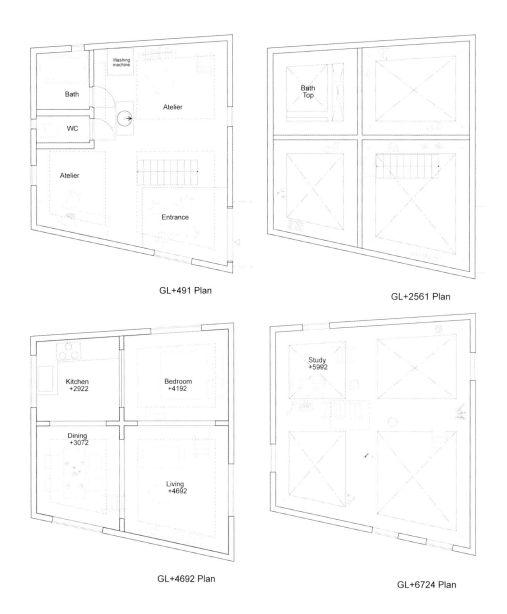

GL+491 Plan

GL+2561 Plan

GL+4692 Plan

GL+6724 Plan

This project is a residence and atelier located in the center of Tokyo.

We created open stage-like floors that resemble bookshelves for this apartment. This design was achieved through the use of intersecting columns.

Residence Tsao

The main concept of this project was to use two rotatable partitions to divide an open space into four distinct areas.

A rotatable partition between the living room and the dining room allows the inhabitants to change the size of the rooms to suit their needs.

The open living area has soft carpet that contributes to the harmonious feel of the apartment. The designer used dark timber for the floor in order to make the lighter objects stand out.

A large bookshelf divides the bedroom and the study. Part of the bookshelf can be moved to the study. This design feature makes it possible to merge the two rooms into a single master suite.

Duplex Refurbishment in Saragossa

This project consists in the complete refurbishment of a duplex apartment inside an existing building in the city of Saragossa, Spain. The client owned this apartment for occasional stays in the city, while his permanent residency is located in Madrid.

The apartment occupies the last two floors of a four-story building with two apartments per floor. Located in a typical suburb, this apartment was built in the early '80s. The apartment had all the materials and finishes typical of its time including old and out of fashion furniture. An integral retrofit was planned, with a complete renovation as the main target, modifying all elements in the house including the distribution, light, design, facilities, etc. The result was completely satisfactory to the client.

The apartment, with a total area of 250 sqm, is accessible through the upper floor. The entry defines the concept and style of all the other spaces. Only a few paintings by Mercedes Rodriguez, a gray carpet, and several metal balls by A-cero break the uniform white. An opening in the ceiling lets the light in through an existing skylight. The project's objective was to make the most of its space, optimize the distribution of the apartment, and simultaneously emphasize the design and light.

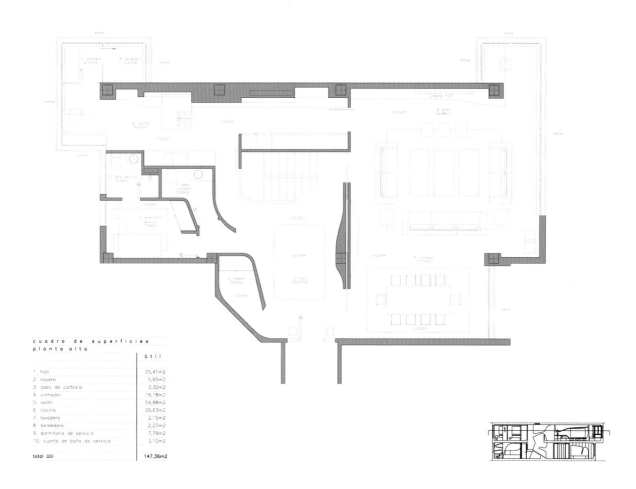

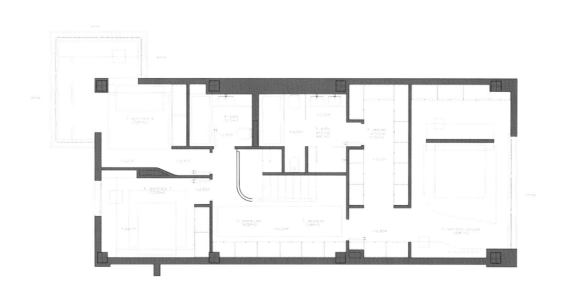

Amida House

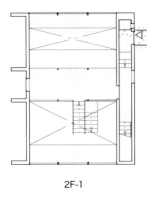

2F-1

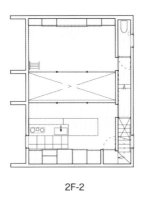

2F-2

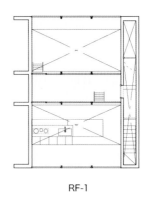

RF-1

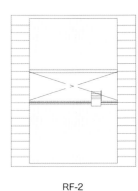

RF-2

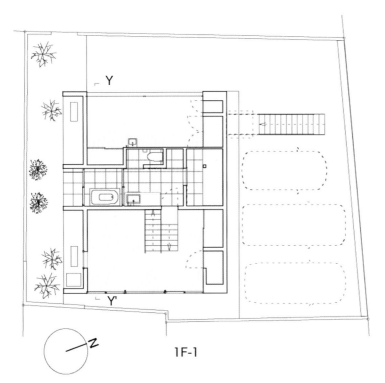

1F-1

Le Corbusier's Domino House has spread all over the world. In a small residence, such a design bisects the space and destroys the relationship between the first and second floors.

The designer decided to use free sections instead of full floors to create a three dimensional relationship in the space. He used the Domino House as a starting point and moved the floors up and down. The result looked like Amidakuji.

The house is located in a residential area in Shizuoka Prefecture in Japan and has a view of Mt. Fuji. The house is compromised of fourteen floors attached at random in a box. Each floor has a different function and a different height.

House in Miyoshi

This house is in Miyoshi City, Hiroshima, Japan. The family home measuring 122.08 sqm is located next to a busy running railway. The building's exterior façade and irregular enclosed space was designed to reduce noise and provide comfort. The kitchen, dining room, and living room are on the first floor. The seating area is on the second floor. The middle of the interior is a high-ceilinged space. This design allows light to enter the first floor.

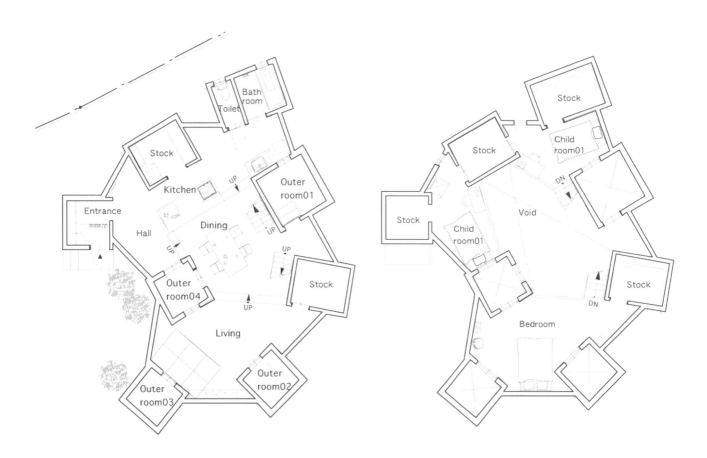

HOUSE IN MIYOSHI HIROSHIMA, JAPAN | SUPPOSE DESIGN OFFICE

House for Three Sisters

This family home is located in a quiet residential area of Tokyo, Japan. Since its construction in the 1950s, the house has undergone a number of extensions to meet the family's changing needs and lifestyle. However, the family finally found it too old to continue to live in without extensive repair and renovation. Because they were very attached to the house, the family decided to reinforce the structure and keep the silhouette and red tiled roof.

In order to create a space where the family members could spend time together, the designers combined the small rooms on the first floor into a single spacious, well-lit living and dining room. The designers placed quake-resistant walls on both sides of a window to secure a large space while reinforcing the structure, which resulted in the void surrounded by those walls. The family plans to use this void as a closet and a computer room. The alcove by the window creates a comfortable light-filled corner. The small computer room in the void makes a perfect work station where one can focus but still feel the presence of the other family members.

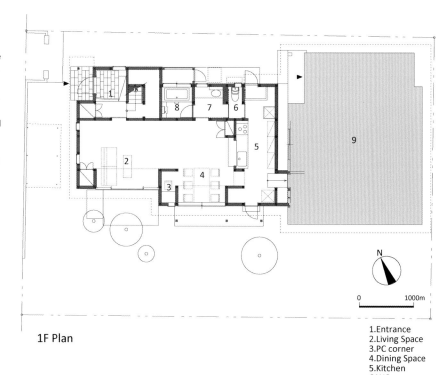

1F Plan

1.Entrance
2.Living Space
3.PC corner
4.Dining Space
5.Kitchen
6.WC
7.Lavatory
8.Bath
9.Existing house

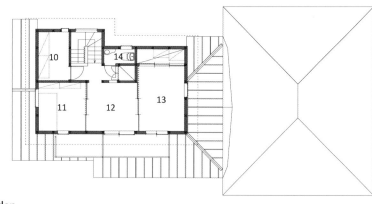

2F Plan

10.Closet
11.Room1
12.Room2
13.Room3
14.WC

House in Megurohoncho

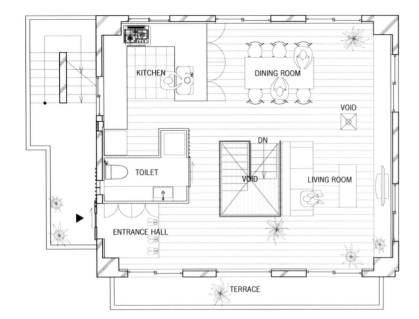

3 F PLAN

2 F PLAN

This project is the renovation of a 40 year-old reinforced concrete building that originally housed storage, office, and residential spaces. The first phase of the project focused on the building's exterior and living quarters. The second phase is set to convert the basement and 1st floor into commercial spaces.

First, all interior partitioning was done away with to free up space. Towering above the surrounding houses, the 3rd floor is well lit and houses the living space, while the 2nd floor offers a more private space. An aperture was made at the center of the 3rd floor and a large piece of furniture with built-in stairs was placed directly underneath it to create a line of flow inside the building. The slightly off-center furnishing loosely partitions the ensemble, and thus creates spaces with different personalities around it.

By integrating new elements with some of the original ones, the designers strove to give the building a unified feel.

INDEX

DIEGO REVOLLO ARQUITETURA

BRAZIL

Revoll Diego, 36, began his studies in Civil Engineering at the Polytechnic School of the University of São Paulo in 1994. He joined the Mackenzie University in 1997 and graduated in Architecture and Urbanism in 2001. He began his career in 2000 working alongside Roberto Migotto and in 2007 opened his own office in Sao Paulo. He won awards in Live Well New Talent (2001), Area D (2006) and Art e-studio (2010). He is attentive to detail and is a perfectionist. He works on the initial design of houses, apartments, shops, and corporate offices to the final choice of objects and works of art. His works have been published in magazines and books in Italy, China, and Japan. He currently serves on the board of Home and Food magazine, published by Editora Globo.

www.diegorevollo.com.br

DOOA ARQUITECTURAS

SPAIN

Dooa Arquitecturas is a young architectural office that started in 2006. Our professional merits: second prize in the Contest of Ideas of the Municipal Patronage of the Housing of Alicante, San Antón's Neighborhood, finalist in the 6th National Contest of Ideas of the Community of Madrid for a day center in Fuencarral, Madrid, first prize in the contest for the construction of a canteen-kitchen in Virgen del Carmen School, Torrevieja, Alicante, Menjarosa, the Menjarosa Build was catalogued by the Foundation Architects' bank between the 128 best accomplishments of young Spanish architects from 2008-2009, and second prize in the contest of ideas for the rehabilitation of Alguazas Old Train Station, Murcia, to name a few.

dooa.es

DRAWING NOTES ARCHITECTS

JAPAN

Drawing Notes Architects was established by Mitsuru Hirai and Sayu Yamaguchi in 2009. Mitsuru Hirai was born in 1974 at Hokkaido, Japan. After withdrawal from the doctoral program, he graduated from Kogakuin University, Graduate School of Architecture in 2009. He was a teacher at Tokyo Technical College and is now a secretary for Docomomo Japan. Sayu Yamaguchi was born in 1985 in Tokyo, Japan. She completed the master course, Department of Housing and Architecture, Japan Women's University.

drawing-notes.jp

ELENBERG FRASER

AUSTRALIA

Elenberg Fraser is not your average architecture firm. An integrated design practice operating across the Asia-Pacific region, their buildings prove that good design leads to economic, social, and cultural benefits. The outcome is sensory – architecture that people can feel, not just see. Elenberg Fraser creates architecture that makes people think and acknowledge the origins of architecture and its plethora of influences, both ancient and modern.

elenbergfraser.com

FACET STUDIO

AUSTRALIA

Olivia Shih and Yoshihito Kashiwagi established Facet Studio in Sydney, Australia in 2008. Facet Studio grew from humble origins: the first project was the renovation of a Thai restaurant. In its 4th year, Facet Studio has gone on to design several Japanese, Vietnamese, and Chinese restaurants in Sydney and has expanded its design portfolio to include retail design, office fit out, single residential, and commercial building. The field of activity has also extended beyond Australia into Japan, China, and France. Due to the number of overseas projects, Facet Studio established an office in Osaka, Japan in 2011 to better care for the projects and clients in Asia, whilst designing and managing from the Sydney office.

facetstudio.com.au

FEDERICO DELROSSO ARCHITECTS

ITALY

An architect with an international range (France, Switzerland, USA, Montecarlo, Turkey), but with a solid Italian grounding, Federico Delrosso (born in Biella in 1964 and graduated from the Milan Polytechnic in 1996) within a few years has gained wide experience in the design of a very wide range of types of architecture: private housing, restaurants, a rehabilitation centre, and office buildings. He has worked on numerous projects of interior design and industrial design.

www.federicodelrosso.com

HIROSHI NAKAMURA

JAPAN

Born in 1974 in Tokyo, Hiroshi Nakamura graduated from Graduate School of Science and Technology, Meiji University in 1999 with a master's degree. From 1997 to 2002, Hiroshi Nakamura worked at Kengo Kuma & Associates. He established Hiroshi Nakamura & NAP Co., Ltd. in 2002.

Hiroshi Nakamura has received numerous awards locally and internationally including AR + D Awards Emerging Architecture 2012 First Prize, Green Good Design Awards, and JIA Young Architect Award to name a few.

www.nakam.info

HIROYUKI SHINOZAKI ARCHITECTS

JAPAN

Hiroyuki Shinozaki was born in Tochigi, Japan in 1978. He graduated from Kyoto Institute of Technology in 2000 and completed the master course at Tokyo National University of Fine Arts and Music in 2002. After that, he started working at Toyo Ito Associates as an architect. He established Hiroyuki Shinozaki Architects in 2009.

www.shnzk.com

I29 | INTERIOR

ARCHITECTS P38-41, P42-47, P48-51

THE NETHERLANDS

We are i29 l interior architects, a creative and versatile interior design studio. Our aim is to create intelligent designs and striking images. Space is the leitmotiv. The result is always clear and we have a keen eye for detail. Our approach is practical yet based on strong ideas articulated in clear concepts. We try to get to the core of things, but keep it looking simple. Our clients are open minded and involved. It is most important to us to enjoy the process together and to get the most out of it!

www.i29.nl

ILA P30-33

THE NETHERLANDS

ILA is a young and dynamic Dutch architecture office that delivers creative and robust spaces within the Netherlands and internationally. Formed by Remi Versteeg and Joost Baks in 2009, we have designed and managed interior design and architectural developments across a wide range of scales and sectors.

Our process when designing for interiors is workshop-driven, maintaining a strong connection with materials, construction, and our network of contractors. This, coupled with our experience of designing buildings in their entirety, allows us to meet the needs of our clients throughout the various phases of a project, enabling us to design and build unique spaces. In addition to our architectural design expertise, we have experience providing consultancy for branding and graphic design.

www.ila.nl

ILMIODESIGN P182-185

SPAIN

ILMIODESIGN is a new creative concept oriented toward the design world in all its aspects. At ILMIODESIGN we address processes of creation from architecture and interior design to industrial and graphic design with a specific methodology. ILMIODESIGN is comprised of a team of experts in the fields of architecture and industrial and graphic design. As a result of this team work and dedication to planning, ILMIODESIGN offers products presented through 3D images, patterns, and complete project execution. We pay special attention to furniture, lighting, and trims to give each project richness.

www.ilmiodesign.com

IÑIGO BEGUIRISTAIN P150-153

SPAIN

Iñigo Beguiristain received his diploma in Architecture in 1998 from the University of Navarre in Pamplona, Spain. He teaches as Associate Professor at the University of the Basque Country. Iñaki Bergera received his diploma in Architecture in 1997 and PhD. in 2002 from the University of Navarre and he currently teaches as Design Professor at the University of Saragossa.

Both Beguiristain and Bergera have been visiting teachers, guest critics, and lecturers at several international universities. They have received several awards in architectural design competitions. Their work in interior design has appeared in many magazines and received several awards.

www.ibeguiristain.com

JOÃO TIAGO AGUIAR P8-13, P52-57, P82-87

PORTUGAL

João Tiago Aguiar was born in Lisbon, Portugal in 1973. He studied architecture in Faculdade Arquitectura Universidade Técnica in Lisboa and graduated in 1996. He collaborated with van Sambeek & van Veen, Amsterdam, Holland, between 1997 and 2000. He collaborated with Broadway Malyan, Portugal from 2000 to 2004. After that, he established João Tiago Aguiar Arquitectos and developed projects in various domains of architecture such as housing, hotels, veterinary clinics, kindergartens, offices, bars, restaurants, shopping, and all sorts of refurbishments. Designing furniture and lighting are also part of the design process of the office. Various projects have already been published in different architecture magazines, architecture blogs, and books.

www.joaotiagoaguiar.com

KC DESIGN STUDIO P114-117, P202-205

CHINA

In order to emphasize the people, activities, and environments in each of our designs, we leave out meaningless decoration and focus on lifestyle, the base environment, and functional composition. We work closely with our clients to produce designs that match their attitudes toward life and their activities.

www.kcstudio.com.tw

KEIJI ASHIZAWA DESIGN P14-17

JAPAN

We try to achieve honest designs through logical thinking. Ideal designs result from the process of attempting to maximize the potential of the clients' ideas, the materials, and functionality. Through the course of my work in production, I realized that it is important to create honest designs through open communication and experimentation with different materials. I use this philosophy in architecture, interior design, production, and furniture design.

www.keijidesign.com

KOCHI ARCHITECT'S STUDIO P212-217

JAPAN

Kochi Architect's Studio was established in 2003 by Kazuyasu Kochi. Kazuyasu Kochi graduated from Tokyo National University of Fine Arts and Music with a master's in architecture in 2000. After graduating he worked at Kazuhiko Namba + KAI workshop. He is now a part-time instructor at Hibaura Institute of Technology, Nihon University, and Tokai University.

www.kkas.net

KRÄF•TE P110-113

JAPAN

Kräf•te is an Osaka-based interior design firm that was established in 2005. We focus on interior design, product design, graphic design, and gallery management. We provide total design solutions from VI development to graphic design and product design.

We use our gallery for exhibition and to propose a means of expressing works.

www.mdnc-krafte.com

LECAROLIMITED P162-167

GERMANY

With an unwavering commitment to creating beautiful solutions for our clients, Lecarolimited delivers designs and creative strategies through a progressive and inquisitive cross-disciplinary practice of architecture, interiors, and production design. Led by Fabian Freytag and Oskar Kohnen, Lecarolimited has delivered solutions that re-imagine the potential in problems since 2005. We work with our clients to re-integrate the spatial concerns of today into a meaningful and responsive outcome. Over the course of the last seven years, Lecarolimited has produced numerous cutting edge projects.

www.lecarolimited.de

LEVEL ARCHITECTS P34-37

JAPAN

We view our role as residential designers as "aiding our clients to give shape to their desires."

Aiding, or planning, has many different meanings and encompasses the environmental and spatial design of the residence. For example, bringing the exterior atmosphere into the interior space to balance the design, solidifying the heart of the house, and organizing the spatial requirements of the family are just a few of the many aspects we focus on. Therefore, communication with the client is our most important task. We develop proposals that reflect our clients' hopes and dreams and add our own special touch.

www.level-architects.com

LKSVDD ARCHITECTS P176-181

THE NETHERLANDS

LKSVDD architects is a creative company with a social conscience. We are architects with vision and courage. We see every project as a challenge to create the best project possible. The office has twenty employees. We work in all sectors including housing, projects, offices, schools, football stadiums, renovation and conversion projects, etc.

www.lksvdd.nl

MINAS KOSMIDIS P102-105

GREECE

For every project we aim to create a proposal that is functionally integral and aesthetically unique. Through an architectural approach, the director creates emotional environments and filters the connection between function and aesthetics, as well as the connection between what is needed and what is wanted.
Using abstraction, line, clarity, transparency, symmetry, flow, balance, nature, and light as tools, he is inspired to create unique projects that combine functionality with a unique aesthetic.

minaskosmidis.com

NUMBER FIVES ARCHITECTURAL DESIGN OFFICE P186-191

JAPAN

Number Fives Architectural Design Office was established in 2005 by Takuya Tsuchida. Born in Fukushima in 1973, Takuya Tsuchida graduated from Kanto Gakuin University in 1996. Before establishing number555, Takuya Tsuchida worked at Maesawa Achitects and TNdesign. Takuya Tsuchida has won various awards. He participated in and was a presenter for Month of Design in Slovenia and is a Good Design Award winner.

number555.com

OFIS ARHITEKTI P76-81

SLOVENIA

Based in Ljubljana, OFIS Arhitekti was formed by Rok Oman and Spela Videcnik in 1998. Rok Oman was born in 1970 and graduated from the Ljubljana School of Architecture in 1998 and from the Architectural Association in London in 2000. Spela Videcnik was born in 1971 and graduated from the Ljubljana School of Architecture in 1997 from the Architectural Association in London in 2000.

www.ofis-a.si

SITE INTERIOR DESIGN P18-23

SOUTH AFRICA

SITE Interior Design is an interior design firm based in the creative capital of Cape Town, South Africa, extending a range of design services specific to residential, leisure, retail, and corporate markets.

We believe that the spatial world is the playground for experience and is shaped by the conviction in the relevance of crafting evocative experiences through the process of thoughtful and considered design. SITE Interior Design is the product of the evolution of our constant refinement of the process of crafting spatial design and of the understanding that the success of a project is contingent on seamless integration of both the exterior and interior designs from the outset.

Ours is a world where interior design fortifies experience and evocative memories linger.

www.siteid.co.za

STUDIO FANETTI P130-133

ITALY

Gianluca Fanetti was born in Bern, Switzerland, in 1973. He trained at the Politecnico di Milano and started his professional career in Italy and Switzerland, where he was involved in several residential projects. He moved to the province of Sondrio in 2003 to found Studio Fanetti. He uses a minimalist language and great attention to detail to bring the dreams and needs of the client to life.

studiofanetti.com

STUDIO_01 P172-175

JAPAN

Studio_01 is a partnership between designers Alex Knezo and Akinori Hamada. Based in Japan in both Tokyo and Toyama, they work on architecture, lighting, furniture, and branding projects. While their designs typically have digitally designed elements, they do not allow the advances in technology to over enhance or over complicate their work. Their design aesthetic typically updates Japanese elements of design without taking them too far into the future.

studiozeroichi.com

SUPPOSE DESIGN OFFICE P218-221

JAPAN

Makoto Tanijiri was born in 1974. In 2000, he started Suppose Design Office, an architectural design firm in Hiroshima. His work covers a broad range of areas including designing houses, business spaces, site frameworks, landscapes, products, and art installations. For the projects, he has collaborated with structural engineers such as Ono Japan and Nawaken Jimu. In 2008, he started a second office in Tokyo. He has since promoted many projects both in Japan and overseas. He recently completed a Toshiba LED light art installation project for Milano Salone 2010. He was awarded the JCD Rookie award and was a finalist in the Heiwa-ohashi Pedestrian Bridge Design Proposal Competition. He is also a part-time professor at Anabuki Design College.

www.suppose.jp

TORAFU ARCHITECTS P228-233

JAPAN

Founded in 2004 by Koichi Suzuno and Shinya Kamuro, TORAFU ARCHITECTS employs a working approach based on architectural thinking. Works by the duo include a diverse range of products from architectural design to interior design for shops, exhibition space design, product design, spatial installations, and film making. Amongst some of their mains works are Template in Claska, NIKE 1LOVE, Boolean, House in Kohoku, and Airvase. Light Loom (Canon Milano Salone 2011) was awarded the grand prize for the Elita Design Award. Airvase Book and Torafu Architects: Idea + Process 2004-2011 were published in 2011. *Torafu's Small City Planning* was published in 2012.

torafu.com

VAILLO + IRIGARAY P150-153

SPAIN

The work of Vaillo + Irigaray is based on a method capable of establishing strategies to cover all scales: from the bench to the city. They have received several national and international awards including the FAD award, COAVN Awards, Award of Merit at ILD Awards, gold medal at Miami Beach Biennial, and the Archizinc award. They were selected to represent Spain at the Helsinki Green Building Challenge.

www.vailloirigaray.com

ACKNOWLEDGEMENTS

WE WOULD LIKE TO THANK ALL OF THE DESIGNERS INVOLVED FOR GRANTING US PERMISSION TO PUBLISH THEIR WORKS, AS WELL AS ALL OF THE PHOTOGRAPHERS WHO HAVE GENEROUSLY ALLOWED US TO USE THEIR IMAGES. WE ARE ALSO VERY GRATEFUL TO MANY OTHER PEOPLE WHOSE NAMES DO NOT APPEAR IN THE CREDITS BUT WHO MADE SPECIFIC CONTRIBUTIONS AND PROVIDED SUPPORT. WITHOUT THESE PEOPLE, WE WOULD NOT HAVE BEEN ABLE TO SHARE THESE BEAUTIFUL WORKS WITH READERS AROUND THE WORLD. OUR EDITORIAL TEAM INCLUDES EDITOR ANNIE LAI AND BOOK DESIGNER CHEN XINWEI, TO WHOM WE ARE TRULY GRATEFUL.